Problem-Based Learning
for Math &
Science

Second Edition

Problem-Based Learning
for Math &
Science

Integrating Inquiry and the Internet

Second Edition

Diane L. Ronis

CORWIN PRESS
A SAGE Publications Company
Thousand Oaks, CA 91320

For information:

Corwin Press
A Sage Publications Company
2455 Teller Road
Thousand Oaks, California 91320
www.corwinpress.com

Sage Publications Ltd.
1 Oliver's Yard
55 City Road
London EC1Y 1SP
United Kingdom

Sage Publications India Pvt. Ltd.
B 1/I 1 Mohan Cooperative Industrial Area
Mathura Road, New Delhi 110 044
India

Sage Publications Asia-Pacific Pte. Ltd.
33 Pekin Street #02-01
Far East Square
Singapore 048763

Printed in the United States of America

Library of Congress Cataloging-in-Publication Data

Ronis, Diane L.
Problem-based learning for math & science : integrating inquiry and the Internet / Diane L. Ronis. — 2nd ed.
    p. cm.
Includes bibliographical references and index.
ISBN 978-1-4129-5558-4 (cloth)
ISBN 978-1-4129-5559-1 (pbk.)
    1. Mathematics—Study and teaching. 2. Science—Study and teaching. 3. Problem-based learning. 4. Internet in education. I. Title.

QA11.2.R66 2008
510—dc22   2007011190

This book is printed on acid-free paper.

07   08   09   10   11   10   9   8   7   6   5   4   3   2   1

Acquisitions Editor:	Hudson Perigo
Editorial Assistant:	Jordan Barbakow
Production Editor:	Astrid Virding
Copy Editor:	Pam Suwinsky
Typesetter:	C&M Digitals (P) Ltd.
Proofreader:	Andrea Martin
Indexer:	Molly Hall
Cover Designer:	Karine Hovsepian

Contents

Preface   **vii**

Introduction   **ix**
   The Concepts Explored in This Book   x
   The Standards Used in This Book   xi
   The Goal of This Book   xiii

Acknowledgments   **xv**

About the Author   **xvii**

Chapter 1: The Integration of Mathematics, Science,
   Technology, and Problem-Based Learning   **1**
   Redefining Literacy   2
   Using Problem-Based Learning to Increase Literacy   6
   Relating Technology to Math and Science   10
   Integrating Problem-Based Learning With
      Cyber-Age Math and Science   13
   Integrated Inquiry Project, Middle Level: Meteorology   15

Chapter 2: Problem-Based Learning
   and Constructivism   **25**
   Why Problem-Based Learning Is Brain Compatible   25
   Problem-Based Learning and the
      Constructivist Model: The Five E's   28
   Teaching in the Problem-Based Learning Classroom   33
   Integrated Inquiry Project, Middle/Secondary
      Level: Developing Entrepreneurial Excellence   38

Chapter 3: Aspects and Approaches of
   Problem-Based Learning   **45**
   Phases of Implementation   45
   Problem-Based Learning Techniques   47
   New Roles for Teachers   56
   Integrated Inquiry Project 1: Middle/Secondary
      Levels: The Roller Coaster   59
   Integrated Inquiry Project 2: Secondary Level:
      Building Bridges   71

**Chapter 4: Planning Problem-Based Learning
   for the Classroom**   **79**
   Planning for Integrated Learning   79
   Guidelines for Implementing a
      Problem-Based Learning Project   81
   Questions to Promote Problem Solving   84
   Integrated Inquiry Project,
      Multilevel: The Mississippi Delta   87

**Chapter 5: Evaluating and Assessing
   Problem-Based Learning**   **93**
   Alternative Assessments   94
   Types of Authentic Assessment and Evaluation   96
   Integrated Inquiry Project,
      Multilevel: Architectural Design   108

**Chapter 6: Integrating Community Learning
   Activities Into the Classroom**   **117**
   The National Association of Partners in Education   118
   Organizational Partnerships in Education   125
   Helping Experts Become Teachers   126
   Community Connections: Multilevel Car Project   128

**Appendix: Cyber Sources for Math,
   Science, and Technology**   **137**

Bibliography   **143**

Index   **149**

Preface

The rapid technological changes of the early twenty-first century, which have fostered a changing economy, require that the population must have a completely different set of job skills than those needed a century or even a decade ago. The kinds of skills that translate into success in current times include critical thinking, problem solving, information literacy, quantitative literacy (numeracy), and self-reliance, as well as the ability to think independently while working collaboratively.

In a constantly changing world filled with ever-increasing challenges, it is the responsibility of teachers to prepare today's students to live and work in a world where they will encounter complex problems on a daily basis. Education must change in basic and crucial ways to equip young people with the skills and attitudes they need to survive and thrive in such an environment. Thus, teachers must fundamentally revise their approach to learning and instruction.

The new understanding of how individuals learn must become the basis for how teachers need to teach. Teachers must move from a teacher-centered perspective to a more student-centered approach. Teachers must shift from presiding over rows of isolated, front-facing students to facilitating collaborative teams of students who face each other; from directing students to collect data on arbitrary topics to encouraging them to investigate questions with direct relevance to their own lives; from leading repetitive memorization and drill of information fragments to guiding students in synthesizing and creating new ideas. These are the skills, attitudes, and abilities students need for success in this twenty-first century, and these are the skills developed in problem-based learning (PBL).

There is something powerfully effective about problem-based learning. In fact, it has proven so effective that medical and professional schools have embraced it enthusiastically. The compelling effectiveness of PBL is in part due to the fact that it ends up orienting students toward meaning making over fact collecting. With PBL, learners must grapple with contextualized problems and situations that employ the dynamics of group work and independent investigation. In this way they are able to achieve higher levels of comprehension, develop more learning and knowledge, and also develop learning and social skills. The PBL approach to instruction brings prior knowledge into play more rapidly and results in the advancement of learning that adapts more easily to new and different situations.

The purpose of *Problem-Based Learning for Math & Science: Integrating Inquiry and the Internet* is to help educators make sense of current research in the brain sciences and the resulting implications for mathematics and science instruction and assessment. Research indicates that an integrated approach to learning aligns with the way the brain naturally processes and internalizes new information. Since mathematics and science are integrated in the world outside the classroom, and technology has become a natural extension of this integration, it seems only logical that these areas be studied together inside the classroom.

As the roles of science, mathematics, and technology grow in society, the corresponding curricula must emphasize a deeper understanding of these topics as well as their relation to each other in the real world. With deep and meaningful learning, students need time for exploring, making observations, testing theories, and redoing; time for building, collecting, and constructing; time for learning whatever mathematics, technology, and science they need to deal with inquiry and problem solving; time for asking questions, wrestling with unfamiliar and counterintuitive thoughts, and learning the advantage of creative thinking.

This book has been constructed to provide teachers with the instructional tools they need to help students learn in an integrated, real-world modality. Through the use of authentic problem situations, methodologics for dealing with messy, confusing, and multifaceted problems, and strategies for issues that have multiple solutions and solution paths, students can learn to tackle real-life problem solving on a daily basis.

However, problem solving alone is no guarantee that learning will take place. Students also need reflection and interpretation to make sense of learning activities and for locating activities in a wider framework of meaning and purpose. In other words, group reflections and self-reflections can be seen as processes in which new personal theories are created or existing ones are modified, and in which new expectations may even be created.

These processes are demonstrated in this book through learning models that encompass implications from neuroscientific and cognitive research, as well as recommendations from the National Council of Teachers of Mathematics (NCTM; 2000) *Principles and Standards for School Mathematics*, the National Science Teachers Association (NSTA), and the International Society for Technology in Education (ISTE). These models integrate technology with self-directed learning and increase student use of higher-level, more sophisticated thinking skills in solving everyday problems.

Today's traditional mathematics classroom remains the only place where learners can be assured of having all the information they need to solve a problem at the outset. It is also the only place where learners can be guaranteed their solution is always the one and only correct solution. This does little to inspire curiosity or to prepare young learners for resolving the intricacies of real-life problems.

An inquiry, problem-based approach to learning, on the other hand, is an approach based upon a teaching philosophy in which the learning process itself is the goal, one in which the individual's quest for knowledge and search for solutions are the learning objectives. These learning goals result in much more than a collection of facts to be memorized. Inquiry instructional strategies effectively turn students into competent problem solvers as well as self-directed, lifelong learners. Such skills can help to successfully prepare students for life and work in the twenty-first century.

Introduction

In the 1980s, the United States moved toward the consensus that its educational system needed to be reformed to meet the demands of an emerging information society—a society that required a workforce able to solve problems, apply knowledge, and reason analytically. To help today's students achieve success, teachers must be able to meet these evolving needs.

When subject areas are taught in a conventional school format, they are taken out of their natural context and presented to learners as independent and isolated units. Unfortunately, this traditional format operates in opposition to the brain's natural way of integrating and processing new information (Ronis, 2007). In mathematics classes especially, information has been taken out of context and is instead taught through the use of examples that show students how to solve problems, then ask students to complete large numbers of similar problems (Ronis, 2006). This process totally ignores the interpretations of current brain research as explained by educators such as Renate Caine, Geoffrey Caine, and C. McClintic (2002); Stanislas Dehaene (1997); Marion Diamond and J. Hopson (1998); Eric Jensen (2005); Robert Sylwester (2004); Pat Wolfe (2001); and James Zull (2002). The research appears to indicate that students (1) develop knowledge through interaction between themselves and the knowledge (active learning), (2) do not think like adults, and (3) learn extremely well through social interaction. When teachers disregard this information about how students actually learn mathematics and instead continue to reinforce drill and memorization, students' broader understanding of mathematical relationships and anything relating to mathematics in general can be harmed.

In the world outside the classroom, subject areas do not occur as separate encapsulated entities. Mathematics, for example, is an integral part of all science because it provides ways to quantify and record observations. Presenting learning and new knowledge in a separate and unconnected manner leads to a lack of student understanding regarding educational institutions and what they stand for. "Why do we need to learn this?" is a question veteran teachers have heard all too often.

The best way for teachers to equip learners with the skills and attitudes they need is through problem solving and inquiry learning (Stonewater, 2005).

Learning should involve the use of inadequately structured "messy" problems, problems that provide only a minimum amount of information—just enough to guide the investigation. These problems and situations cross subject boundaries and cannot predictably be solved using algorithms or formulas.

Inadequately structured, open, complex problems evolve as more information is gathered and often conclude with more than one solution. Student-directed inquiry serves as the heart of this problem-solving process. When students wrestle with the intricacies of such problems, they begin to discover what it is they need to know to arrive at an acceptable solution. Once in possession of this knowledge, they can then determine how to locate the information they need. This process allows students to learn to become effective and self-directed problem solvers and also to develop the ability to work collaboratively.

The problem-solving process has been expanded through technology that allows access to mathematics and science that could not be explored in the past. Theoretical mathematics models that could previously only be imagined can now be constructed using sophisticated software and computers. Difficult scientific models and experiments can be simulated in much the same manner. Technology helps create environments in which students can see changing relationships among variables and can engage in conjecture in a dynamic way. It allows students to tackle real problems with "messy" data and gives them control over different forms of representational relationships.

The workforce of the future will need a high level of technical skill: computers will continue to be used for tasks such as word processing, controlling machines, analyzing complicated sets of data, conducting research, and ensuring quality control in production processes. Current academic preparation in mathematics and science barely touches on these skill areas. As stated in the National Research Council report, *Mathematical Preparation of the Technical Workforce* (Mathematical Sciences Education Board, 1995):

> Mathematics in the workplace is quite different from mathematics in school. It is more concrete and more intuitive, yet at the same time more exciting and more unpredictable. It is rich in data and inextricably linked to technology. To become adults capable of thriving in the new workplace, students must be active learners and collaborative problem solvers. (p. 5)

As learners enrich the range of connections and relationships among different styles of absorbing, associating, and applying information, they form more intricate neural pathways in their brains, and concept retention increases. When learners are able to see otherwise abstract concepts functioning in their familiar world, a significant learning link is forged.

THE CONCEPTS EXPLORED IN THIS BOOK

This book examines the rationale behind inquiry and problem-based learning (PBL). Why is this exploratory method of learning so effective for mathematics and science education? How can problem-solving activities be made messier and brought closer to home so as to capture student interest and forge significant learning links? How might such learning be evaluated? And how might technology be made as much an integral part of education's inquiry process as it is currently part of real-world problem solving? This book also helps teachers design units that engage students in the exploration of important ideas, ideas that deepen understanding through their relevance and meaning to the learner.

PBL problems can vary widely as to the degree and level of teacher direction versus student direction. Starting with the greatest amount of teacher control and ending with the most student direction, the various types of PBL problems include:

- Teacher-directed PBL, in which the teacher selects the knowledge to be taught, creates the learning environment, develops and uses the evaluation materials, and presents the problem. This kind of PBL most resembles the traditional classroom.

- Real-life-referenced PBL, in which the problem evolves from an authentic situation, as in the environmental project presented in Chapter 4 of this book, The Mississippi Delta Dilemma.

- Simulation of a real problem, as in Chapter 3, where students are directed to create their own roller coasters and bridges.

- Student-community problems, where PBL can facilitate students' learning how to conduct a real-life decision, as in the car project discussed in Chapter 6, in which students decide which car to buy after gathering information from local car dealerships and banks.

THE STANDARDS USED IN THIS BOOK

The standards used for the projects in this book are based on standards from the National Council of Teachers of Mathematics *Principles and Standards for School Mathematics* (NCTM, 2000), the National Science Education Standards (NSES), the International Society for Technology in Education (ISTE), and the National Education Technology Standards (NETS) Project. Each project starts with a list of relevant standards related to the age group targeted for that project.

The intent of the mathematics, science, and technology standards can be expressed in a single phrase: mathematics, science, and technology standards for all students. An educational paradigm shift toward these standards is urgent, due to the manner in which society has recently evolved. Commerce now functions in a worldwide arena filled with fierce international competition, while technology has become an essential part of people's daily lives. In spite of the excitement and innovation that has accompanied this dynamic state of affairs, the current educational system in the United States remains under attack for its lack of substance and relevancy (*Trends in International Mathematics and Science Study* [TIMSS], 2003). Educators, policymakers, parents, and the community at large are asking themselves, "Just how are we failing our children?" By using a standards guideline, a collective outlook can be formed as to what quality education looks like, today and in the future. The current standards movement offers a coherent vision for the future, defining excellence for performance as well as content standards in the various subject areas. These standards apply to all students, regardless of age, gender, cultural or ethnic background, disabilities, aspirations, and intent and motivation.

Standards-based instructional policies are essential for the evolution of the current educational system. Traditionally, new concepts have been presented as disconnected fragments that create an inherently inconsistent curriculum through which students study a series of isolated ideas. What is now known about learning demonstrates that if these new concepts are not in some way connected to previously learned concepts, they cannot become enduring or meaningful to the learners (Caine & Caine, 1997a, 1997b). Standards help connect learned concepts to new concepts by building a bridge between what is known and what is to be learned.

The NSES (science) standards integrated throughout this book state that teachers of science should do the following:

- Plan an inquiry-based program for their students
- Guide and facilitate their students' learning
- Engage in ongoing assessment
- Design and manage learning environments that provide students with the time, space, and resources needed for learning science
- Develop communities of science learners that reflect the intellectual rigor of scientific inquiry and the attitudes and social values conducive to science learning

The International Society for Technology in Education, an organization committed to addressing the development and application of knowledge through its National Educational Technology Standards Project, lists technology foundation standards that are reflected throughout this book. These include the following:

- Technology as productivity tools
- Technology as communication tools
- Technology as research tools
- Technology as problem-solving and decision-making tools

The NCTM standards for mathematics from *Principles and Standards for School Mathematics* (2000) stress problem solving as a meaningful method of inquiry and application. This is principally due to the following:

- Problem solving is the process by which students experience the power and usefulness of mathematics in the world around them.

- Problem solving can establish a "need to know" and foster motivation for development of the concepts.

- A balance must be established between problems that apply mathematics to the real world and problems that arise from the investigation of mathematical ideas.

- Computers and calculators, as powerful problem-solving tools, can help students become independent doers of mathematics.

- The nonroutine problem situations envisioned are different from traditional word problems, which provide contexts for using particular formulas and/or algorithms, but do not offer opportunities for problem solving.

- Students need to work together frequently in small groups to discuss strategies and solutions, ask questions, examine consequences and alternatives, and reflect on the process and how it relates to prior problems.

While students achieve understanding in diverse ways and at various levels according to their interests and abilities, all students can develop the knowledge and skills described in the various standards. In fact, some students will achieve well beyond those levels.

Mathematics, science, and technology standards rest on the premise that learning is an active process. Learning mathematics and science is something students do, not something that is done to them, and technology provides the tools for students to learn. Hands-on activities, while essential, are not enough in and of themselves. What students really need to ensure their success is "minds-on" experience.

THE GOAL OF THIS BOOK

This book is intended for educators interested in strengthening student understanding and comprehension in the fields of mathematics and science. The use of technology skills and tools as well as the creation of new instructional models and designs are the keys to accomplishing this goal.

The book does not suggest that all instruction be constantly geared toward deep and sophisticated understanding. There are many instances (such as the mastering of multiplication facts or chemistry element symbols) where such depth is neither desirable nor feasible. Rather, this book is about the understanding that once those basic skills have become a part of the learner's vocabulary, a more sophisticated understanding of the subject can be achieved only through direct participation in meaningful inquiry and discovery. Traditional teaching methods are not to be discarded, but PBL should be used to enhance, strengthen, and expand the educator's repertoire to increase student success.

Each of the six chapters in this book outlines an aspect of PBL as it relates to math and science. At the end of the chapters, projects designed to engage learners in the PBL experience are provided. Each project opens with a list of the project standards as they relate to math, science, and technology covered in the project, and also includes the information, student handouts, and evaluation forms necessary for completion. These projects can be modified to suit various learning levels.

The ideas and concepts of PBL are explored in each chapter in the following ways:

- Chapter 1 explores the concept of an integrated, inquiry-based approach to mathematics and science, and discusses why these subjects should be taught in this manner, how technology provides the glue for this learning, and how teachers can best use such exploratory methods in the classroom. The chapter closes with a multilevel meteorology project.

- Chapter 2 explains why problem-based (inquiry) learning is relevant and how it relates to current brain research on how students learn best. This chapter also includes a multilevel entrepreneurial project.

- Chapter 3 discusses ways in which PBL can be implemented to synthesize mathematics, science, and technology and make them more creative, relevant, and global. Two secondary-level projects dealing with real-world mathematics and physics are also offered.

- Chapter 4 provides strategies for implementing PBL in the math and science classroom and offers a multilevel environmental project.

- Chapter 5 offers information on alternative assessment and evaluation measures. Samples of different rubrics are provided as well as sample self-evaluations and reflections for both group and individual work. This chapter contains a multilevel practical applications project dealing with architectural design.

- Chapter 6 introduces the concept of community-embedded mathematics and science activities, offers ways teachers can engage the community as a learning resource, and explains how such activities can be initiated as well as integrated into classroom learning. In this chapter, the multilevel project gives students the opportunity to interact with the local business community.

Acknowledgments

Corwin Press gratefully acknowledges the following reviewers:

April Keck DeGennaro
NK–8 Teacher
Fayette County Board of Education
Fayetteville, GA

Sandra K. Enger
Associate Professor of Science Education
The University of Alabama in Huntsville
Huntsville, AL

Debra Gerdes
Professional Development Leader for Problem-Based Learning
Illinois Mathematics and Science Academy
Aurora, IL

Sally Koczan
Sixth Grade Science Teacher
Wydown Middle School
Clayton, MO

Katie Morrow
Technology Integration Specialist
O'Neill Public Schools
O'Neill, NE

Beverly R. Plein
Technology Facilitator
Benjamin Franklin Middle School
Teaneck, NJ

About the Author

 **Diane L. Ronis** is currently a professor of education at Southern Connecticut State University and holds a PhD in curriculum and instruction. She has been involved in the field of education since 1968 and has been a keynote speaker and presenter at numerous conferences and workshops throughout the country. Her area of expertise is in the transferring of neuroscientific research into practical strategies that classroom teachers can easily implement.

As a new professor in 1998, she began creating material for her classes that would be in keeping with her vision for cutting-edge, high-quality instruction and assessment methodologies that teachers would find easy to understand and implement. These materials evolved into the five books she has published: *Clustering Standards in Integrated Units*; *Critical Thinking in Math*; *Problem-Based Learning for Math & Science: Integrating Inquiry and the Internet*; *Brain-Compatible Assessments*; and *Brain-Compatible Mathematics*.

The Integration of Mathematics, Science, Technology, and Problem-Based Learning

Problem-based learning (PBL) is based on the idea that individuals fashion their understanding largely through what they experience. This inquiry method of learning allows learners to process and acquire new information in the way most suited to their natural brain processes.

During PBL, research is conducted and various strategies are explored with the end goal of developing practical, logical, and relevant solutions to "messy" problems that have been incompletely structured. The skills students gain from taking part in PBL activities are essential for their future success. The rapid technological changes in today's society make it critical for students to develop the ability to conceive of ideas and solutions to problems and situations that may be unfamiliar to them.

Teachers can incorporate PBL into learning experiences through the use of ill-constructed problem or project units. These units consist of problems that simply do not have enough information to be solved. Researching the missing information helps students understand what is occurring and also helps them decide what actions (if any) are required for resolution. In PBL tasks, the teacher's role is that of facilitator and coach rather than leader. The teacher's job is to make sure the problem directions are thoroughly understood by students before the project begins, provide research sources to students, and facilitate group work that takes place in the classroom. Teachers are not always in complete control of the learning during PBL, since students take responsibility for their own knowledge acquisition.

There is no single correct way to conduct a PBL investigation, as each problem is unique and evolves as new information is found. In addition, because students make their own decisions and create their own solutions to these problems, there are often many correct paths to completion.

REDEFINING LITERACY

Literacy refers to a basic competency in a given area. For example, reading literacy is the ability to read at a functional level. As society moves toward the future, traditional ideas of literacy in subject areas are changing. The definition of literacy is expanding to include aspects of technology and problem-solving skills.

Although students should achieve literacy in all subject areas by the time they graduate from high school, traditional teaching methodologies do not integrate literacy concepts well enough to allow them to attain this goal. PBL encourages learners to become literate by allowing them to use standards in various contexts to solve problems. Such hands-on experience in applying different concepts to diverse problem situations furthers the learner's literacy. Literacy in mathematics, science, and technology is not optional for this new generation of learners; it is a requirement for future success (Wilkins, 2000). As the world becomes increasingly dependent on technology, only those individuals who possess the skills to work collaboratively as well as independently, who are good communicators and able to make informed decisions, and who successfully exhibit the skills of critical thinking and problem solving will succeed.

Mathematical Literacy

Quantitative literacy, or *numeracy*, means different things to different people. Although quantitative literacy is often confused with its close relatives such as basic skills, elementary statistics, logical reasoning, or advanced mathematics, none of these offers a complete or balanced view of numeracy by themselves (Steen, 1990, 1997). Quantitative literacy is both more than and different from mathematics as traditionally viewed by school and society. Many basic mathematical skills are essential for numeracy, including arithmetic, percentages, ratios, simple algebra, measurement, estimation, logic, data analysis, and geometric reasoning. But also essential are concepts not normally emphasized in traditional school mathematics (Forman & Steen, 1999), such as the following:

- Estimating tolerances and errors
- Simulating complex systems on computers
- Using flowcharts for planning and management
- Drawing inferences appropriately (statistical, scientific, logical)

- Presenting data-based arguments by using modern computer tools
- Thinking, visualizing, and calculating in three dimensions

The real test of literacy, be it quantitative or qualitative, is whether a person naturally uses appropriate skills in many contexts. Thus, students need to learn numeracy in multiple contexts, such as economics and biology or history and geography. Unfortunately, mathematics is traditionally isolated from the rest of the curriculum, and high-school mathematics especially focuses on preparing only those students who intend to enter professions that require calculus (Wilkins, 2000). If all high-school graduates are to be quantitatively literate, teachers must encourage students to see and use mathematics in everything they do: for measurement in science, for logic and reasoning in language and communication, for ratios and rhythms in music, for geometry in art, and for scoring and ranking in athletics. Teachers in all subjects, not just mathematics, must help students think of mathematics not only as tasks on school worksheets, but as something that arises naturally in many different contexts (Price, 1997).

The best way for teachers to emphasize the versatility of mathematics is to use real-world problem situations that employ mathematics to reach a solution or conclusion. These should be relevant problems that use mathematics much the way professionals use mathematics every day. Learners can then see exactly why fluency in mathematics is necessary for them to be informed and knowledgeable citizens in today's world.

Scientific Literacy

According to the National Academy of Sciences and the National Science Teachers Association, science literacy consists of a knowledge of certain important scientific facts, concepts, and theories; the exercise of scientific habits of mind; and an understanding of the nature of science, its connections to mathematics and technology, its impact on individuals, and its role in society. To achieve such goals, students need time to acquire the essential knowledge and skills of science literacy. They need to explore fewer topics in greater depth so as to gain an understanding of the scientific process and ways of thinking scientifically. All students must be frequently and actively involved in exploring nature in ways that resemble how scientists work.

In a classroom where science literacy is the goal, teaching should not be rushed. To truly learn science, students need time for exploring, making observations, realizing inconsistencies and wrong turns, testing ideas, and doing things over; time for building things, collecting things, and constructing physical and mathematical models for testing ideas; and time for learning whatever math, science, and technology they need to tackle the question at hand.

In a world filled with the products of scientific inquiry, scientific literacy has become a necessity for everyone. We all need to use scientific information to make choices that arise every day. We all need to be able to engage intelligently in public discourse and debate about important issues that involve science and technology. Scientific literacy is of increasing importance in the workplace as well. More and more jobs demand advanced skills, requiring that people be able to learn, reason, think creatively, make decisions, and solve problems. An understanding of science and the processes of science contributes in an essential way to these skills. The National Science Education Standards (NSES) present a vision of a scientifically literate populace. They outline what students need to know, understand, and be capable of to be scientifically literate at different grade levels.

Technical Literacy

Technical literacy usually refers to basic competency with computers, which necessitates the ability to understand technology through the underlying science and mathematics principles. Components of technical literacy include the following:

- Operational competence with modern technology systems
- The ability to evaluate and use a variety of common technology applications
- The ability to innovate and invent ways of applying technology in challenging new situations
- An understanding and sensitivity to societal issues related to technology

In the past, technical literacy included programming, use of tools such as word processors and spreadsheets, use of Web browsers and Web search engines, and construction of Web sites. But unlike most forms of literacy, technical literacy is changing rapidly, and soon many of these capabilities in their current forms will be outmoded and replaced. Technical literacy, therefore, presents its own special problems in that teachers often find that the approaches they are trained for are outmoded. Teachers can combat this problem by staying at a cutting-edge skill level and taking part in a high-quality professional development program. In the current educational system in the United States, it is up to individual teachers to keep their technical skills as current as possible. The best way for teachers to do this is to become involved in a problem-solving instructional approach that uses the Internet as a primary research source.

Written and Oral Communication Literacy

As evidenced by the fact that written and oral communication continue to be a National Council of Teachers of Mathematics (NCTM) standard, as well as a standard from the NSES, the role of communication remains an important aspect of math and science comprehension.

In its 1989 wake-up call document, *Curriculum and Evaluation Standards for School Mathematics,* the NCTM took the position in unequivocal terms that new goals in mathematics education were needed. The shift in the United States from an industrial to an information society had affected both the mathematics students needed to be taught and the concepts and procedures students needed to master in order to function as productive citizens in the future. The NCTM recommended that one of education's new goals be to develop mathematically literate workers flexible enough to become lifelong learners. The NCTM still retains this goal of helping young people develop abilities that enable them to understand underlying mathematical aspects of problems and communicate and work with others on such problems (National Council of Teachers of Mathematics [NCTM], 2000). The standards document summarized the changes in instructional practice with increased attention to:

- Problem solving as a means as well as a goal of instruction
- Student communication of mathematical ideas orally and in writing
- Use of a variety of instructional formats (small group, individual explorations, peer instruction, whole-class discussion, project work)
- Use of calculators and computers as tools for learning and doing mathematics
- Systematic maintenance of student learnings; embedding review in the context of new topics and problem situations
- Assessment of learning as an integral part of instruction (NCTM, 2000)

Writing is important in helping students understand math and science concepts because it helps students communicate their thinking and solidify their conceptual understanding. It develops a student's abilities to read, define, and hypothesize. It includes methods of problem solving, increases knowledge (particularly metacognitive awareness), recognizes attitudes, and promotes collaboration.

Writing is also a highly effective instrument for developing problem-solving skills. Various writing approaches promote the type of thinking and reasoning needed for good problem solving. Some examples of how writing can be used to develop these methods include the following:

- Writing out problems and solutions
- Designing investigations or describing how to solve a problem
- Comparing and contrasting alternative approaches
- Describing how to use technology in problem situations

Composing and evaluating within the writing process promotes learning in ways similar to mathematics problem solving or scientific inquiry. Writing activities encourage students to formulate the goals and plans needed to address the assigned task. In carrying out those goals through narrative, students engage in metacognitive processes that extend and develop their thinking about math and science. In evaluating their writing, students contemplate and refine their approaches to and conclusions about important concepts, ideas, and situations. Writing encourages students to move back and forth between these stages and enables them to be conscious of the strategies they use to understand information (National Council of Teachers of English [NCTE], 1996). Teachers can use writing to reinforce learning during a PBL experience by asking students to write an explanation of the steps they followed to reach their conclusion and to reflect upon the validity of that conclusion. Or teachers can ask students to write an initial hypothesis and then revise that hypothesis as new information modifies their thinking.

USING PROBLEM-BASED LEARNING TO INCREASE LITERACY

PBL helps teachers teach for literacy in several ways. According to Finkle and Torp (1995):

> PBL is a curriculum development and instructional system that simultaneously develops both problem solving strategies and disciplinary knowledge bases and skills by placing students in the active role of problem-solvers confronted with an ill-structured problem that mirrors real-world problems. (p. 1)

Specific tasks in a PBL environment include:

1. Determining whether a problem exists

2. Creating an exact statement of the problem

3. Identifying information needed to understand the problem

4. Identifying resources for gathering information

5. Generating possible solutions

6. Analyzing the solutions

7. Presenting the solution, orally and/or in writing

Steps 2 through 5 may be conducted concurrently as new information becomes available and redefines the problem. Stage 6 may occur several times during the course of solving the problem.

PBL engages students in learning, thus helping them become more literate in subject areas. This idea is based on several theories of cognition. Two such prominent theories are that students are best motivated to work on problems they perceive as being meaningful or relevant (Caine, Caine, & McClintic, 2002), and that "it is a basic and pervasive human need to invent meanings, and to invest meanings in one's world. It [is] a property of the human mind to search for and to find significance everywhere, to transform experience constantly to uncover new meanings" (Gardner, 1983, p. 50).

Norman and Schmidt (1992) state that there are three roles for PBL. The first is the acquisition of factual knowledge, the second is the mastery of general principles or concepts that can be transferred to solve similar problems, and the third is the acquisition of prior examples that can be used in future problem-solving situations of a similar nature.

With the PBL process, it is important that students learn and acquire concepts while they are actively wrestling with the problem. It is vital to the process that students receive corrective feedback about the solution immediately upon completion. Constructive feedback, as much as ongoing assessment, reinforces learning.

When creating ill-structured problems, teachers must keep in mind that in a well-constructed problem situation, students need more information than what is initially presented to them. Missing information helps students understand what is occurring and also helps them decide what actions (if any) are required for resolution. The teacher, as guide and facilitator, helps to point out that the information provided is insufficient and that the students' job is to search for the missing components. There is no right way or fixed formula for conducting a PBL investigation, since each problem is unique, and the problem continually changes as new information is found.

Some of the projects used in this book are highly authentic and are reflective of real-life situations and concerns, while others appear to be more contrived and teacher directed. This is primarily because state curricula dictate the subject areas to be covered in all classrooms. While authentic problem situations can be designed so that most of a subject area is covered, complete coverage often dictates the need for some contrived situations and thereby necessitates more teacher direction to ensure total coverage.

As exciting and stimulating as PBL is, problems can occur at times during the process implementation. Some of the possible difficulties that might occur include the following:

- Students familiar with a traditional classroom may at first be uncomfortable with the PBL format. It is the teacher's job to convince students to think of themselves as researchers looking for information and solutions to problems that may not have only one right answer. It is often helpful if teachers remind students that professionals in the real world frequently deal with problems that have unclear solutions. Teachers should point out that often these professionals must become detectives in their quest for problem solutions.

- Students may want to know what they "really" have to do to get their grade. They may expect the teacher to spoon-feed them by prescribing a number of tasks, events, concepts, or work to be completed. In this situation, it is easier if teachers explain beforehand that this project or unit will be different from previous units. Teachers should explain that in this project or unit, students will act as researchers, and for that reason, their goal is to do research. Teachers should stress that students must learn this new information independently as well as with their teammates and then analyze and synthesize the new information into a final product that they design and create.

- Students adept at "book learning" may feel uncomfortable in PBL roles in which they have to conduct research, coordinate with peers, and generate unique products. These students' parents may express some concern when their child isn't comfortable with this new environment. At this point it is extremely beneficial for teachers to point out that the teacher's role is to prepare students to be successfully functioning adults and that the skills of problem solving are essential for success in the world beyond school.

Teachers can facilitate the PBL process by becoming metacognitive coaches, serving as models, thinking aloud with students, and modeling behavior they want their students to use (Delisle, 1997). Teachers should help students become comfortable with such metacognitive questions as: What is going on here? What do we need to know more about? What did we do during the problem that was effective? Teachers coax and prompt students to use questions and take responsibility for the problem. Over time, students become self-directed learners, and teachers can then provide less scaffolding, fading into the background. This view of self-directed learning as vitally important is embraced by Papert (1996), who believed that when a child is "taught" a concept, he or she is deprived of the "pleasure and benefit" of discovery. When young learners are enthusiastic about a fact or concept they themselves have discovered, they better retain the new information and use it in creative and meaningful ways.

This constructivist approach to learning contends that people learn best by doing rather than simply by listening. *Inquiry learning* and *problem-based learning* are both terms used to describe this type of learning, and in fact they mean the same thing. A problem-based approach to learning requires the use of inquiry since it is based upon the idea that knowledge is best acquired through the investigation and resolution of problems. This inquiry/solution learning methodology prepares students by letting them tackle real-life issues—the same issues professionals deal with on a daily basis.

Inquiry and PBL techniques help develop higher-order critical thinking skills. Critical thinking skills are analytical skills that allow individuals to think logically using information based on sound evidence (the opposite of biased, sloppy thinking). The word *critical* has a number of different meanings. It means analytical, and it means evaluative or judgmental, but it also means indispensable, vital. Critical thinking supports and encourages increased comprehension and academic performance by involving students in the use of skills requiring analytical thinking. It is only through the repeated use of skills such as comparing and contrasting or classifying and sequencing that students can begin to use logic and understand how it works. Some of the logical and critical thinking skills used in inquiry and PBL are the following:

- Comparing and contrasting
- Classifying and sequencing
- Drawing analogies
- Strategy planning
- Drawing inferences and predicting outcomes
- Determining cause and effect
- Following and writing directions
- Critical reading and content analysis for discernment of meaning and clarity of thought
- Mapping and directionality
- Use of Venn and branching diagrams (flowcharts, matrices, and webs)
- Identifying and creating patterns and symmetry
- Mental manipulation of objects
- Deductive and inductive reasoning as well as logic
- Analyzing, evaluating, synthesizing, and interpreting
- Applications to the world outside the classroom

In addition to these reasoning skills, questioning strategies are also used to help students discuss and debate new and unfamiliar concepts and ideas. Questioning strategies reinforce thinking processes that are used to write about or carry out sophisticated learning tasks so that students can internalize the learning, thereby increasing the likelihood that they will be able to transfer the knowledge.

Self-reflective assessment activities are used to guide student metacognition (the thinking about and analysis of work done). Metacognition encourages the transfer of thinking skills into other appropriate contexts to help develop a pattern of lifelong learning.

Some of the questioning and metacognitive strategies that can be used during PBL units to encourage students to think with greater care are the following:

- Higher-order questioning (questioning that necessitates a reflective answer based on analysis, synthesis, and evaluation, such as "Compare the processes of multiplication and division of fractions and explain why the fraction gets larger as a result of the division process")
- Socratic dialogue (using a questioning technique to help students arrive at their own conclusions, for example, "If a roller coaster has no engine, what propels the cars after the first hill?")
- Analytical reading (the process of reading a passage critically for the information within it, and then breaking that information down into digestible pieces)
- Strategic writing (writing that follows a definite sequence or logic; writing that defines a particular goal)
- Cooperative learning (learning that involves cooperation among team members to achieve a particular goal, with each team member performing his or her part for the good of the team)
- Use of manipulatives (learning materials students can work with physically, thereby affording them the opportunity to understand an abstract concept using concrete objects)
- Graphic organizers (outlines that help to graphically organize pertinent information)

Since problem-based instructional methods are student centered rather than teacher centered, problem based rather than solution based, and inductive rather than deductive, they differ from more traditional forms of math or science instruction. In the traditional, deductive, teacher-oriented approach, the teacher poses the theorem, postulate, or rule to the class and then gives the students examples to reinforce their understanding (passive learning). With the problem-based inductive format, the teacher gives the students information and asks them to develop the questions that must be answered to move toward a solution. For math and science learning to be truly inquiry based, the problems must be realistic, relevant, and authentic (real world) so that students can relate to the context. For learners to become engaged in problem-solving activities, they need to see the purpose behind the work.

Since PBL uses inductive reasoning, the teacher provides the students with a minimum of information—only those facts most vital to the investigation.

The problem presented should be unambiguous in that its parameters and requirements are clearly stated in language that is understandable and appropriate for the circumstances. The goal of this problem solving is in the exploration and research aspects rather than only in finding the solution. Instead of supplying students with a prescribed strategy, the inquiry/problem-solving approach expects students to discover the mathematical principles embedded in the real-world problems they are solving. Students must solve problems using their prior knowledge and by experimenting with new ideas. The teacher's role is to ask questions that guide and build students' understanding.

RELATING TECHNOLOGY TO MATH AND SCIENCE

Technology is the "glue" that enables learners to approach mathematics and science from a more global perspective, because technology offers students the tools and information they need to explore math and science connections in the real world. Through technology, the gathering and interpreting of information has become greatly simplified. Teachers and students can quickly transport data from CD-ROMs and the Internet into spreadsheets, word processing programs, and multimedia presentations, or they can view these data from the computer screen using a projection system. Graphing calculators and spreadsheets help students understand the statistics used in making predictions and inferences. By using technology, students practice math and science skills. For example, students tap into their geometric and problem-solving skills when doing Web design, hone information-finding skills when conducting Internet research, and engage in problem-solving skills when using spreadsheet programs to plug in data.

Technology supports and facilitates conceptual development, exploration, reasoning, and problem solving by empowering students and teachers to investigate questions that reflect their own interests.

The following principles, which were adapted from a report submitted to the National Science Foundation (Flores, Middleton, Knapp, & Staley, 1997), provide a general view of technology standards.

1. Technologies are instruments educators should use. While such instruments cannot supplant students' thought processes, they certainly can reinforce them.

2. Technologies should enable students to do what they could not do without them (for example, engage in scientific experiences not feasible with other tools).

3. Technologies must be on hand all the time so that when the need arises, students can integrate them into their learning.

4. Technologies should allow students to develop, refine, and test materials and scientific phenomena. Thus, they should facilitate the creation of information students can share, modify, and transport elsewhere.

5. Technological systems should be user-friendly, making it easy for students to share data and resources.

6. Computer placement and the classroom environment in general should increase communication among students, not stifle it.

7. Technologies must engage students in independent exploration.

These standards are always part of a quality PBL situation. They help to integrate technology and the learning experience in a manner that is natural rather than contrived. As such, technology is used in the classroom much as it is used in the world beyond the classroom.

According to the International Technology Education Association (ITEA), technology education is best described as applied human knowledge or "human innovation in action." In its 1995 document, *Technology for All Americans: A Rationale and Structure for the Study of Technology,* the ITEA explained that through the study of technology, students learn to extend their human capabilities by way of designing, inventing, innovating, practical problem solving, producing, communicating, and transporting.

The National Educational Technology Standards for Students

Today's educators must address using technology as a tool for applying content knowledge in authentic contexts. Students must be able to apply knowledge for the construction of new understanding, problem solving, decision making, exchanging information, connecting ideas, product development, and communication. The International Society for Technology in Education (ISTE) is an organization committed to addressing the development and application of such knowledge, and has created the National Educational Technology Standards (NETS) Project.

The NETS for students were developed with support from the U.S. Department of Education, National Aeronautics and Space Administration (NASA), the Santa Monica–based Milken Exchange on Education Technology, and Apple Computer. Many professional education groups have also joined as project partners. The National Council for Accreditation of Teacher Education (NCATE) will use these standards to establish technology competency for K–12 students as well as to recommend applications of technology for use in all areas of the K–12 curriculum.

The four primary National Educational Technology Standards are the following:

1. *Technology Foundations Standards:* These describe what students should know about technology and be able to do with technology.

2. *Standards for Using Technology in Learning and Teaching:* These describe how technology should be used throughout the curriculum.

3. *Educational Technology Support Standards:* These describe systems, access, staff development, and support services schools should provide.

4. *Standards for Student Assessment and Evaluation for Technology Use:* These describe means of assessing and evaluating the use of technology in learning and teaching.

Educators can use the NETS as a guide in recognizing and addressing conditions leading to effective use of technology in K–12 education. The standards serve as a guide in assisting educational leaders in recognizing and addressing those conditions leading to effective use of technology support for K–12 education. The specific NETS competencies for technological literacy listed following for various grade levels reflect the technological abilities modeled throughout the projects in this book.

Prior to completion of second grade, technology literate students will:

- Use multimedia resources (interactive books, educational software, and elementary multimedia encyclopedias) to support learning
- Work cooperatively and collaboratively with peers, instructors, and others when using technology in the classroom
- Use technology resources (puzzles, logical thinking programs, writing tools, digital cameras, drawing tools) for problem solving, communication, and illustration of thoughts, ideas, and stories

Prior to completion of fifth grade, technology literate students will:

- Use telecommunications to access remote information, to communicate with others, and to pursue personal interests
- Use telecommunications and online resources (e-mail, online discussions, Web environments) to participate in collaborative problem-solving activities
- Determine when technology is useful and select the appropriate tools and technology resources to address tasks and problems

Prior to completion of eighth grade, technology literate students will:

- Use content-specific tools, software, and simulations (environmental probes, graphing calculators, exploratory environments, Web tools) to support learning and research
- Apply multimedia tools and peripherals to support personal learning throughout the curriculum
- Collaborate with peers, experts, and others using telecommunications and collaborative tools to investigate curriculum-related problems, issues, and information and to develop solutions or products for audiences inside and outside the classroom
- Select and use appropriate tools and technology resources to accomplish tasks and solve problems
- Demonstrate an understanding of concepts underlying hardware, software, and connectivity, and of practical applications to learning and problem solving

Prior to the completion of twelfth grade, technology literate students will:

- Routinely and efficiently use online information resources for collaboration, research, publications, communications, and productivity

- Select and apply technology tools for research, information analysis, problem solving, and decision making in content learning
- Investigate and apply expert systems, intelligent agents, and simulations in real-world situations
- Collaborate with peers, experts, and others to contribute to a content-related knowledge base by using technology to compile, synthesize, produce, and disseminate information models and other creative works

INTEGRATING PROBLEM-BASED LEARNING WITH CYBER-AGE MATH AND SCIENCE

By its very nature, the problem-based approach to math and science requires an organizational framework similar to detective work. By first identifying specific focus questions and then proceeding through systematic research for answers, students learn the discipline of logic along with the excitement of mental connections that click, resulting in insight and epiphany. Technology helps teachers make interdisciplinary connections by providing access to worthwhile data. In addition, technology facilitates an in-depth explanation of mathematical and scientific topics previously thought too complex for typical classrooms, especially when they involve real-world, messy data. The ready availability of Internet access allows teachers and students to quickly gather real-world information for their inquiries.

Ubiquitous Internet comes at an exciting juncture in American education reform. The urgent need for and emphasis on "interactivity" in the learning process is directly linked to the idea that each learner actively creates his or her own knowledge through direct and meaningful experience.

Neuroscientists who have been studying the effects of enriched environments on rats' behavior for years support this idea. Some of the best and most current work is that of Greenough and his colleagues at the University of Illinois (Greenough, Briones, & Klintsova, 2004). These neuroscientists studied the way raising rats in different environments affects the rats' brain structure. Other studies in monkeys and humans have established that the adult brain remains highly plastic and capable of extensive neural reorganization throughout life. The brain's ability to reorganize itself in response to new experiences is what makes it possible for individuals to learn throughout their lives. The new view of learning draws its strength from cognitive neuroscience, cognitive psychology, and artificial intelligence, and can best be expressed through the following statements:

- Learners conduct understanding for themselves.
- To understand is to know relationships.
- Knowing relationships depends on having prior knowledge.

Most researchers believe that all conscious and subconscious knowledge and behaviors are constructed as complex systems within the brain. "[While] the individual constructs basic knowledge through experience, the quality of the construction depends on how well the brain organizes and stores the relationships between and among aspects in the events" (Lowery, 1998, p. 27).

Lowery (1998) goes on to say that with so much explicit knowledge about how the brain works and with data clearly supporting the fact that students construct knowledge for themselves, it is surprising so little real change has occurred in the way science and math are taught. And it is even more surprising that some educators see no need to change from overusing passive-learner instructional methods to implementing more thoughtful methods that enable students to construct meaning for themselves through exploring relationships and webbing those explorations to their prior knowledge.

Such knowledge about how the brain learns best is actively considered in an interactive school, where students communicate with each other through formal presentations, cooperative learning activities, and informal dialogue. Students and teachers communicate about their learning tasks in large groups, small groups, and one to one. Students have constant access to and know how to use print and electronic information resources to inform their learning activities. They recognize the value of the information sources in their own communities and interact with community members to receive authentic information from primary sources.

Also related to knowledge about the brain is the idea that teaching strategies and curricula that help students connect math and science to the real world can also affect how students perform in math and science classrooms. When encouraged to work in cooperative groups, when given opportunities to communicate their understandings (both verbally and in writing), and when evaluated through an assortment of assessment tools and strategies, students become less apprehensive and more positive about their abilities to "do" math and science.

"Math anxiety," a term often used to refer to the negative outlook many students have toward mathematics, can be eased in situations in which students can see math's real-world applications, and when the class goal is cooperation instead of competition (Stonewater, 2005).

In most traditional classrooms, math is presented in a very logic-based, detached manner, which appeals to relatively few students. While more progressive and constructivist teaching methods are starting to be used in the science classroom, mathematics classrooms lag far behind. Integrating math with scientific inquiry in the way it often occurs outside the classroom allows students to see the relevancy of both subjects. In this way, mathematics and science appeal to a wider range of learning styles, thereby increasing the number of students who realize they are capable of learning advanced mathematical and scientific principles.

When students explore information through a variety of different instructional approaches, they often become more interested in and receptive to the subjects they are studying. Because the brain is functioning with greater efficacy through these varied approaches, students are able to invest more of their mental energy in learning and thereby commit concepts to memory with greater comprehension. When information is isolated from systems that manipulate, visualize, and interpret, that information is forgotten and becomes inaccessible to memory (Cowley & Underwood, 1998). When students are given the chance to articulate and share their thoughts, they are able to develop a more sophisticated understanding of a subject's meaning and relevance.

Teachers can give their students the opportunity to explore information in a PBL manner through the following project.

INTEGRATED INQUIRY PROJECT, MIDDLE LEVEL: METEOROLOGY

The following weather/meteorology task is set up for middle-level instruction. However, it can be adapted to elementary and secondary levels, depending upon the sophistication and depth of the research involved. Teachers are provided with background information on various aspects of meteorology and can choose which topics they would like their students to research. The goal of the project is for students to conduct research on one of the topics and present it to the class or the teacher (for example, through a presentation or written report). The teacher decides how research results should be presented.

To gear this project toward elementary students, teachers should have students concentrate on researching clouds and precipitation along with the hydrologic cycle (the natural sequence through which water passes into the atmosphere as water vapor, precipitates to Earth in liquid or crystal form, and ultimately returns to the atmosphere through evaporation).

Project Standards (Grades 6–8)

I. Mathematics Content Standards (Adapted From the National Council of Teachers of Mathematics, 2000)

Standard 1: Numbers and Operations

Instructional programs from pre-kindergarten through grade 12 should enable all students to

- Compute fluently and make reasonable estimates

Standard 3: Geometry

Instructional programs from pre-kindergarten through grade 12 should enable all students to

- Use visualization, spatial reasoning, and geometric modeling to solve problems

Standard 4: Measurement

Instructional programs from pre-kindergarten through grade 12 should enable all students to

- Understand attributes, units, and systems of measurement
- Apply a variety of techniques, tools, and formulas for determining measurements

Standard 5: Data Analysis and Probability

Instructional programs from pre-kindergarten through grade 12 should enable all students to

- Develop and evaluate inferences and predictions that are based on data

Standard 6: Problem Solving

Instructional programs from pre-kindergarten through grade 12 should enable all students to

- Build new mathematical knowledge through problem solving
- Solve problems that arise in mathematics and in other contexts
- Apply and adapt a wide variety of strategies to solve problems
- Monitor and reflect on the process of mathematical problem solving

Standard 7: Reasoning and Proof

Instructional programs from pre-kindergarten through grade 12 should enable all students to

- Select and use various types of reasoning and methods of proof

Standard 8: Communication

Instructional programs from pre-kindergarten through grade 12 should enable all students to

- Organize and consolidate their mathematical thinking through communication
- Analyze and evaluate mathematical thinking and strategies of others

Standard 9: Connections

Instructional programs from pre-kindergarten through grade 12 should enable all students to

- Recognize and apply mathematics in contexts outside of mathematics

Standard 10: Representation

Instructional programs from pre-kindergarten through grade 12 should enable all students to

- Create and use representations to organize, record, and communicate mathematical ideas
- Select, apply, and translate among mathematical representations to solve problems
- Use representations to model and interpret physical, social, and mathematical phenomena

II. Science Content Standards (Adapted From the *National Science Education Standards*, 1995)

Content Standard A: Science as Inquiry

Students should develop:

- Abilities necessary to do scientific inquiry
- Understandings about scientific inquiry

Content Standard B: Physical Science

Students should develop an understanding of:

- Motions and forces
- Transfer of energy

Content Standard D: Earth and Space

Students should develop an understanding of:

- Structure of the Earth system

Content Standard E: Science and Technology

Students should develop:

- Abilities of technological design
- Understandings about science and technology

Content Standard F: Science in Personal and Social Perspective

Students should develop an understanding of:

- Populations, resources, and environments
- Natural hazards
- Science and technology in society

III. Technology Foundation Standards (International Society for Technology in Education [ISTE]) (Adapted From the *National Educational Technology Standards (NETS) Project*, 1998)

Basic Operations and Concepts

- Students demonstrate a sound understanding of the nature and operation of technology systems.
- Students are proficient in the use of technology.

Technology Productivity Tools

- Students use technology tools to enhance learning, increase productivity, and promote creativity.
- Students use productivity tools to collaborate in constructing technology-enhanced models, preparing publications, and producing other creative works.

Technology Communications Tools

- Students use telecommunications to collaborate, publish, and interact with peers, experts, and other audiences.
- Students use a variety of media and formats to communicate information and ideas effectively to multiple audiences.

Technology Research Tools

- Students use technology to locate, evaluate, and collect information from a variety of sources.
- Students use technology tools to process data and report results.
- Students evaluate and select new information resources and technological innovations based on the appropriateness to specific tasks.

Technology Problem-Solving and Decision-Making Tools

- Students use technology resources for solving problems and making informed decisions.
- Students employ technology in the development of strategies for solving problems in the real world.

Performance Task

Students are to conduct research on the hydrologic cycle and present that information to the teacher or the class. Teachers can read the information in Figure 1.1 with students or present it to them in a handout.

Figure 1.1   Background Information for Meteorology Project

Water is the source of all life on Earth. The distribution of water, however, is quite varied; many locations have plenty of it while others have very little. Water exists on Earth as a solid (ice), liquid, or gas (water vapor). Oceans, rivers, clouds, and rain—all of which contain water—are in a frequent state of change (surface water evaporates, cloud water precipitates, rainfall infiltrates the ground, and so on). However, the total amount of Earth's water does not change, because it continues to circulate from one place to the other. The circulation and conservation of Earth's water is called the "hydrologic cycle."

Meteorologists in the modernized National Weather Service (NWS) are taking on increased hydrologic duties. Although each office works with a Service Hydrologist, these people are able to cover only 5 out of 21 shifts each week. Therefore, forecasters need to be prepared to address hazardous hydrologic conditions and generate flood forecasts, especially in headwater basins (basins at the source of a stream), where the response times can be very short.

A headwater forecast process can be generalized into four steps.

1. Most of the time spent on hydrology-related functions during a meteorological forecast shift is allocated to the first step, the Hydrologic Watch, where data are collected and evaluated to determine if there is a potential hydrologic event in small streams in local Hydrologic Service Areas (HSAs).

2. When an event appears likely, the next step is Quality Control and Additional Data Collection.

3. Next, Hydrologic Analysis is carried out using the tools available for the location of concern.

4. The final step is a return to the Hydrologic Watch with the additional task of monitoring the issued product for accuracy.

Thus, the forecast process is a continuous loop. Most Weather Forecast Offices (WFOs) produce one or more routine hydrologic forecast products for their HSA each day based on site-specific guidance received from one or more River Forecast Centers (RFCs).

Project Instructions

Teachers should hand out the instructions in Figure 1.2 to students, and also read and discuss them with the entire class. Teams can begin their research at the various sites listed in the Resources, which are arranged by level. All these sites contain information on the phases of the hydrologic cycle, such as evaporation, condensation, transport, and so forth.

Figure 1.2   Meteorology Project Instructions

Your class has been assigned to intern as five research teams at a local weather station. A series of storms is due to hit the area shortly. Two teams have the assignment of categorizing the kinds of storms that are common to the area and providing background information on those same storm types for the weather announcer. Another of the teams is to contact the Tropical Prediction Center for details of recent storms. Meteorologists at the Tropical Prediction Center work to monitor hurricane systems as they move, issuing hurricane watches and warnings with adequate time for the public to prepare. Meteorologists and the public rely on these hurricane hunters to learn more about the hurricane. Two additional teams will research the El Niño phenomenon and find out if any of the recent storms can be linked to this phenomenon. Teams can begin their research at the site or sites provided by the teacher. These sites contain information on the phases of the hydrologic cycle, such as evaporation, condensation, and transport.

Resources

Elementary-Level Weather Research

http://ww2010.atmos.uiuc.edu/(Gh)/guides/mtr/hyd/home.rxml
The Online Meteorology Guide, designed by the Department of Atmospheric Sciences at the University of Illinois, offers information on all aspects of the hydrologic cycle.

http://www.ec.gc.ca/water/en/nature/prop/e_prop.htm
This site, published by Environment Canada, contains information on the nature of water, the hydrologic cycle, quick facts, and links to related sites.

Middle-Level Weather Research

http://ww2010.atmos.uiuc.edu/(Gh)/guides/mtr/home.rxml
This section of the Online Meteorology Guide, which is designed by the Department of Atmospheric Sciences at the University of Illinois, contains information relating to atmospheric sciences.

Secondary-Level Weather Research

http://meted.ucar.edu/index3.htm
MetEd's (Meteorological Education and Training) homepage contains discussion, resources, links, and case studies focusing on meteorology-related subjects.

http://meted.ucar.edu/topics_hydro.php

This Web site contains the COMET® program's first online hydrology training module for meteorologists. The newest COMET Web-based module describes a generalized process for monitoring hydrologic conditions and deciding whether to issue flood watches and warnings for small streams and headwater basins.

http://meted.ucar.edu/topics_convective.php

This Web site deals with upper-level weather prediction techniques. It shows students how to develop a method that consistently predicts the motion of both right- and left-moving supercells (using only a hydrograph), allows them to compare the new method with existing methods of predicting supercell motion, and recommends a preferred method for predicting supercell motion.

Research Extension Activities

The following Web site (the Middle-Level Weather Research Web site) contains instructional units teachers can use for extension units with students who are not sufficiently challenged by the class assignment or students who complete the assignment well in advance of the rest of the class. Teachers can encourage students to develop their own research topics after reviewing the sites.

http://ww2010.atmos.uiuc.edu/(Gh)/guides/mtr/home.rxml

This site contains a collection of Web-based instructional units that use multimedia technology and the dynamic capabilities of the Web. These resources incorporate text, colorful diagrams, animations, computer simulations, audio, and video to introduce fundamental concepts in the atmospheric sciences. Selected pages link to relevant classroom activities and current weather products to reinforce topics discussed in the units and allow the user to apply what has been learned to real-time weather data.

The units available on the Web site that can be used as extension projects include the following:

- *Light and Optics:* The interaction between light and atmospheric particles and the colorful optical effects that result
- *Clouds and Precipitation:* Cloud classifications and the processes by which clouds and precipitation develop
- *Forces and Winds:* Forces that influence the flow of air and how they interact to produce wind
- *Air Masses and Fronts:* The most common types of air masses and fronts, plus a look at the different types of advection (horizontal air movement)
- *Weather Forecasting:* General forecasting methods, important surface features, plus forecasting tips for different scenarios
- *Severe Storms:* Different types of thunderstorms and the components associated with them, plus an in-depth look at tornadoes
- *Hurricanes:* The anatomy of hurricanes, how they develop, and why they are dangerous
- *El Niño:* Why El Niño develops and the global impact it has on weather patterns and economics
- *The Hydrologic Cycle:* The cycle of circulation and conservation of Earth's water

The summaries that follow are descriptions of the Online Meteorology Guide links to the units mentioned. Teachers can use these summaries to decide if they want to do an extension project with their students on one of the topics.

Light and Optics

http://ww2010.atmos.uiuc.edu/(Gh)/guides/mtr/opt/home.rxml

This unit investigates particle-light interactions and the assortment of optical effects (such as rainbows, sunsets, and halos) they produce. The Light and Optics unit has been organized into the following sections:

- *Mechanisms:* Particle/molecule-light interactions responsible for creating optical effects. These interactions include reflection, scattering, refraction, and diffraction.
- *Air, Dust, and Haze:* Optical effects resulting from the interaction of light with air, dust, and haze particles. These effects include crepuscular rays, blue skies, blue haze, and sunsets.
- *Ice Crystals:* Optical effects resulting from the interaction of light with water droplets. These effects include cloud iridescence, rainbows, and the silver lining along the edge of clouds.

Clouds and Precipitation

http://ww2010.atmos.uiuc.edu/(Gh)/guides/mtr/cld/home.rxml

The purpose of this unit is to introduce students to a number of cloud classifications, different types of precipitation, and the mechanisms responsible for producing them. The Clouds and Precipitation unit is organized into the following sections:

- *Development:* Refers to the importance of rising motion and the mechanisms responsible for lifting the air
- *Cloud Types:* Includes high-, middle-, and low-level clouds, vertically developed clouds, and some less common cloud types
- *Precipitation:* Deals with rain, snow, hail, sleet, and freezing rain

Forces and Winds

http://ww2010.atmos.uiuc.edu/(Gh)/guides/mtr/fw/home.rxml

The purpose of this unit is to introduce pressure and discuss how it changes with height and the importance of high- and low-pressure systems. In addition, the unit introduces the pressure gradient and Coriolis forces and their role in generating wind. Local wind systems such as land breezes and sea breezes are also introduced. The Forces and Winds unit has been organized into the following sections:

- *Pressure:* Introduces pressure and its associated characteristics and high- and low-pressure centers
- *Atmospheric Pressure:* Force exerted by the weight of the air, defined as the force per unit area exerted against a surface by the weight of the air above that surface

- *Pressure Gradient Force:* A net force that is directed from high to low pressure
- *Coriolis Force:* The apparent deflection of objects due to Earth's rotation
- *Sea Breezes:* Atmospheric conditions that lead to the development of sea breezes
- *Land Breezes:* Atmospheric conditions that lead to the development of land breezes

Air Masses and Fronts

http://ww2010.atmos.uiuc.edu/(Gh)/guides/mtr/af/home.rxml

The purpose of this unit is to introduce air masses, where they originate, and how they are modified. Clashing air masses in the middle latitudes spark interesting weather events, and the boundaries separating these air masses are known as *fronts.* This unit examines fronts and offers detailed explanations about cold fronts and warm fronts. Finally, different types of advection are introduced, such as temperature, moisture, and vorticity advection. The Air Masses and Fronts unit has been organized into the following sections:

- *Air Masses:* Masses that commonly influence weather in the United States
- *Fronts:* Boundaries separating air masses; includes warm fronts, cold fronts, occluded and stationary fronts, and dry lines
- *Advection:* Introduces these horizontal air movements and describes the differences between warm and cold advection

Weather Forecasting

http://ww2010.atmos.uiuc.edu/(Gh)/guides/mtr/fcst/home.rxml

Weather forecasts provide critical information about the weather to come, and in severe weather situations can help save lives and protect property. This unit introduces forecast methods and the numerous factors a person must consider when attempting to make an accurate forecast. The Weather Forecasting unit has been organized into the following sections:

- *Forecasting Methods:* Different forecasting methods for different weather scenarios
- *Surface Features:* Important surface features to consider when making a forecast
- *Forecasting Temperatures:* Factors to consider when forecasting day and nighttime temperatures
- *Forecasting Precipitation:* Factors to consider when forecasting precipitation

Severe Storms

http://ww2010.atmos.uiuc.edu/(Gh)/guides/mtr/svr/home.rxml

The Severe Storms unit is a combination of two elements. The first is the National Oceanic and Atmospheric Administration (NOAA) Severe Storms

Spotters Guide. The second discusses the efforts and results of modeling severe storms. The Severe Storms Spotters Guide contains supplemental instructional resources and a program designed to familiarize meteorologists and advanced severe storm spotters with the basic "building blocks" of convective storm structure. The focus of this unit is the development of a thunderstorm "spectrum" and a discussion of the physical characteristics and severe weather potential of the various storm types in the spectrum. The Severe Storms unit has been organized into the following sections:

- *Dangers of Thunderstorms:* Lightning, floods, hail, winds, and tornadoes
- *Types of Thunderstorms:* Single cells, multicell clusters, multicell lines (squall lines), and supercells
- *Components of Thunderstorms:* Updrafts and downdrafts, outflow phenomena, wall clouds, and the effects of wind shear on thunderstorm development
- *Tornadoes:* Cyclic storms and low-level flow fields associated with tornadic thunderstorms
- *Modeling:* Supercells, squall lines, and other phenomena re-created inside computers for the benefit of forecasting and understanding

In this unit, the critical role of atmospheric dynamics and thermodynamics in determination of storm type is stressed, examining the storms that range from the small summer storms capable of producing dangerous "microbursts" to the large "supercell" storms that spawn destructive tornadoes.

Hurricanes

http://ww2010.atmos.uiuc.edu/(Gh)/guides/mtr/hurr/home.rxml

The purpose of this unit is to introduce hurricanes and their associated features and discuss where they develop and under what conditions. The Hurricanes unit is organized into the following sections:

- *Definition and Growth:* Defining a hurricane and explaining where and how they develop
- *Stages of Development:* From depression to hurricane
- *Structure of a Hurricane:* Different parts of hurricanes
- *Movement:* The influence of global winds on the movement of hurricanes
- *Satellites and Hurricane Hunters:* The tools and means meteorologists use to observe and track hurricanes
- *Preparations:* Factors to consider when a hurricane threatens
- *Damage and Destruction:* Features associated with hurricanes, plus the Saffir-Simpson Scale for classifying any damage potential
- *Global Activity:* Regions of Earth where tropical cyclones can be found
- *El Niño:* The manner in which El Niño appears to affect hurricane activity

El Niño

http://ww2010.atmos.uiuc.edu/(Gh)/guides/mtr/eln/home.rxml

This unit introduces El Niño, the cause of the conditions responsible for its occurrence, and the impact it has on the rest of the world. The El Niño unit has been organized into the following sections:

- *Definition:* Introduces El Niño, discusses when El Niño events have been recorded and how it compares to La Niña
- *Upwelling:* Introduces upwelling and the thermocline and how they affect local sea life populations
- *Non–El Niño Years:* Discusses typical oceanic and atmospheric conditions that exist in the tropical Pacific when El Niño is not present
- *El Niño Events:* Explores conditions that lead to an El Niño event and discusses how El Niño influences upwelling processes, tropical rainfall, and local fish populations
- *Sea Surface Temperatures:* Offers El Niño visualized through sea surface temperature anomaly plots
- *Impacts on Weather:* Discusses the influence of El Niño on weather conditions worldwide
- *Economic Impacts:* Refers to reduction in local fish populations, which in turn affect local industry and market prices worldwide
- *Detection and Prediction:* Deals with methods and resources used by NOAA for detecting and predicting the presence of El Niño

The Hydrologic Cycle

http://ww2010.atmos.uiuc.edu/(Gh)/guides/mtr/hyd/home.rxml

This unit examines the natural sequence that water passes through when it passes into the atmosphere as water vapor, precipitates to Earth in liquid or crystal form, and ultimately returns to the atmosphere through evaporation. The Hydrologic Cycle unit is organized into the following sections:

- *The Earth's Water Budget:* Discusses the distribution of water among the oceans, land, and atmosphere
- *Evaporation:* Explores the transformation of water from a liquid to a gas
- *Condensation:* Discusses the transformation of water from a gas to a liquid
- *Transport:* Looks at the movement of water through the atmosphere
- *Precipitation:* Explores the transfer of water from the atmosphere to land
- *Groundwater:* Examines water located beneath the ground
- *Transpiration:* Looks at the transfer of water to the atmosphere by plants and vegetation
- *Runoff:* Discusses how rivers, lakes, and streams transport water from land to oceans

Problem-Based Learning and Constructivism

Problem-based learning (PBL) is effective in teaching students because it reinforces the characteristics of brain-compatible learning. Recent cognitive and neuroscientific research has created the basis for this "science" of teaching by showing that learners learn best when they are engaged in the learning, which is the process that occurs during a PBL activity.

WHY PROBLEM-BASED LEARNING IS BRAIN COMPATIBLE

Constructivist learning theory explains why learning may not always be the outcome of good teaching and suggests instructional strategies that are consistent with what researchers know about the ways in which students learn.

Students learn best by using the following, which are all part of a constructivist approach:

- A multiplicity of learning approaches
- Active rather than passive participation in the construction of new knowledge
- Extra processing time for metacognitive activities (knowledge assimilation and reflection)
- Emotional, intellectual, and physical connections to the content
- Socialization within a safe environment that encourages risk taking

Several principles regarding cognition (Caine & Caine, 1994, 1997a, 1997b; Sylwester, 2005) have been found to be true that are in line with constructivist theory, such as the following:

- New information cannot be transmitted as personally meaningful knowledge by the actions of a teacher "on" a learner. Equating teaching with signal transmission and learning with passive reception undermines meaningful learning. Meaningful learning occurs only when new information can be connected to a student's prior knowledge in a way that encourages flexible and creative expression in new and different situations.

- Learning is an active, constructive process in which the individual selectively perceives, filters, organizes, transforms, and responds to sensory experiences through the modification of internal cognitive structures. Learning means creating new links to prior knowledge. It is a process of building conceptual bridges as connections between what is already understood and what needs to be learned.

- Students are not blank slates or sponges; they contain a considerable amount of prior knowledge (as well as neurological sophistication and capabilities) from other less formal learning settings. This personal "meaning making" has the following characteristics:

  1. It begins at birth and continues over a lifetime. The drive to "make sense" and achieve mastery is innate; it doesn't necessarily have to be externally motivated by rewards and/or punishments such as gold stars or grades. People learn best when they have questions they want answered. Effective teachers tap into this natural drive to know and be able to do by addressing the often unspoken student questions: So what? Who cares?

  2. It is likely to be intuitive and qualitative; students may not even be consciously aware of their mental processing and/or faulty conceptions. Academic performance can be improved through metacognitive awareness training and monitoring.

  3. It is highly personal; no two people ever experience and mentally process a given event in exactly the same way. One of the benefits of cooperative learning is that articulation and discussion of diverse viewpoints provides multiple perspectives to enrich conceptual understandings and reasoning skills.

  4. It is subtle and often overlooked by teachers or, if noticed, may seem incoherent or self-contradictory. For the individual student, knowledge is organized as "internal concept maps" or *schemata* (psychological webs of interconnected pieces of information).

  5. It strongly influences what can be learned from new experiences.

Most traditional learning methodologies by their very nature do not foster meaning making. Traditionally, subjects, topics, and concepts have been taught in isolation, as disassociated bits and pieces of information to be categorized and memorized. By using problem or project units that are relevant to students' lives and that are real-world based, students are able to make the connections between the new information and their established knowledge. Mastery of basic facts and skills does not always have to precede meaningful, conceptual learning and critical or creative thinking skills. In fact, thinking skills should be given primary attention throughout the instructional process.

While current cognitive and neuroscientific research may appear to imply that all people are innately curious, socialization and emotionality are also vital components to comprehension and enduring knowledge (Ronis, 2006). Learning is social and collaborative, and thus is enhanced when the environment provides learners with the opportunity to discuss their thinking out loud, to bounce their ideas off their peers, and to produce collaborative work (Wolfe, 2001). Emotion also plays a vital role in human learning. It plays a positive role in that the stronger the emotion connected with an experience, the stronger the memory of the experience. Therefore, when emotional input is added to the learning experience, it becomes more exciting and more meaningful, and the brain deems the information more important, thereby increasing retention (Wolfe & Brandt, 1998). Inquiry methods pose problems for students to solve, and the best way for students to find solutions to these problems is in small-group settings in which the social and emotional aspects of learning are also encouraged.

Brain-Compatible Characteristics of Problem-Based Learning

The current shift toward cognitive psychology and brain-compatible learning has educators increasingly interested in helping students develop and learn thinking strategies. The problem-based instructional approach follows brain-compatible learning recommendations (Ronis, 2006) in the following ways:

- Learners must feel safe and secure before meaningful learning can occur. The school environment must foster a feeling of security, for complex learning is enhanced by challenge and inhibited by threat. In other words, the learning environment in the classroom must represent a low level of frustration or stress while at the same time providing a high level of challenge.
- The brain is social, and learning thrives in group situations.
- The search for meaning is innate, and problem-solving situations allow the brain to make use of this inborn drive.
- Since the brain searches for meaning through patterning, and emotions are critical to patterning, the more a learner is emotionally as well as socially involved with his or her work, the greater the amount of learning retained for future application.
- Group work fosters student learning since the brain simultaneously perceives and creates parts and wholes. In group work, a project can be dealt with as an entity and at the same time as the individual contributions that make up that entity.

While cognitive research and neuroscience do not definitively prove that any particular strategy or method of instruction is better than another, this research does help teachers better understand how the brain does or doesn't learn, and why. Researchers are beginning to gain a scientific understanding of the learning process, and from that understanding teachers are able to make better decisions about how to structure learning environments and instructional practices. PBL and inquiry learning methods are in line with what researchers have found about how the brain learns best.

Instruction and Brain Development

The brain stores information, but exactly what kind of information does it preserve? Neuroscientists are not the ones addressing these questions; rather it is the cognitive scientists, educational researchers, and others who study the effects of experience on human behavior and human potential. Neuroscientific research is beginning to provide some insights, if not final answers, to questions that are of great interest to educators. There is growing evidence that both the developing and mature brains are structurally altered when learning occurs. Thus, these structured changes are believed to encode the learning brain (National Research Council, 2000). These findings suggest that the brain is a dynamic organ, shaped, to a great extent, by experience—by what an individual does and has done.

As a result of this new and deeper understanding of the brain, educational leaders have made some recommendations to promote a more brain-compatible style of teaching and learning in schools, which can be accomplished through the use of PBL and inquiry learning methods. These recommendations include the following:

- Teachers provide variety and stimulation for students through the use of projects, field trips, speakers, and varied media.
- Teachers have students actively conduct inquiries and research, create products, and make presentations or exhibitions using their interests as a springboard for the project concepts.
- Teachers act as facilitators, coaches, arrangers, expediters, or stage managers.

Comprehension is most readily achieved through relationship construction (making connections), application and extension of an individual's existing knowledge (inquiry and research), and an individual's ability to reflect on his or her experiences to the extent that he or she can then articulate the new understanding (metacognition).

PROBLEM-BASED LEARNING AND THE CONSTRUCTIVIST MODEL: THE FIVE E'S

Constructivism is a learning philosophy that proposes that learners need to build their own understanding of new ideas. Since PBL is a methodology in which learners are actively constructing their own knowledge, the PBL philosophy is in essence a constructivist philosophy. Much about this learning philosophy has been researched and written by eminent leaders in the fields of learning theory and cognition. Scholars such as Jean Piaget, Eleanor Duckworth, George Hein, and Howard Gardner, to name a few, have explored these ideas in depth. Piaget

(1954), for example, described cognitive development in terms of stages from birth to maturity. These cognitive stages presuppose a maturation process in the sense that development is a continuation based on previous growth. Piaget felt that environmental experience was key based on the following three cognitive processes: (1) assimilation, which is incorporation of new experiences into existing experiences; (2) accommodation, whereby the child's existing cognitive structures are modified and adapted in response to the environment; and (3) equilibrium, the process of achieving balance between things previously understood and things yet to be understood. Eleanor Duckworth (1979) supports the constructivist learning theory by stating that much knowledge can be learned through the use of probing questions that direct students in their learning.

The Biological Science Curriculum Study (BSCS) has developed an easily implemented instructional model for constructivism, or helping learners build their own understandings of new ideas, called the "Five E's," consisting of Engagement, Exploration, Explanation, Elaboration, and Evaluation (Trowbridge & Bybee, 1995).

The principal idea of the Five E's model is that teaching a concept must be a recursive or spiral experience rather than a one-shot operation. This means that to achieve meaningful learning and comprehension of a subject, students must encounter a subject that engages their multiple intelligences numerous times. The term *multiple intelligences* was coined in 1983 by Howard Gardner, who proposed that individuals possess some aspects of all seven innate intelligences: verbal/linguistic, visual/spatial, logical/mathematical, bodily/kinesthetic, musical/rhythmic, interpersonal, and intrapersonal. In 1993, Gardner expanded his theory to include an eighth intelligence, the naturalist intelligence.

One way teachers can teach a unit as a spiral experience is to assign a student-designed survey and have students carry out the assignment as a team. Students can choose a survey topic and gather their data through interviews (use of interpersonal intelligence). Then, they can collate and analyze the data (use of logical/mathematical intelligence) and synthesize and create graphic representations of the data (use of visual/spatial and bodily/kinesthetic intelligences). Teams develop their results and conclusions through research and reflection (use of intrapersonal intelligence).

Engagement

In the Engagement stage, learners first encounter and identify their instructional task. It is in this phase that teachers must help students make connections between past and present learning experiences, lay the organizational groundwork for the activities ahead, and activate student involvement in these activities in anticipation of the learning activities. Asking a question, defining a problem, showing a surprising event, and acting out a problematic situation are all ways teachers can engage students and focus them on the instructional tasks. Concept mapping, asking puzzling questions, and using audiovisuals, simulations, and discrepant event-type demonstrations are additional ways teachers can engage students. The goal here is similar to that of marketing professionals: to grab the customer's attention. This doesn't occur unless the customer thinks he or she has a need to buy the product. If the customer is unaware of such a need, the marketer must create the need.

Students take part in the following steps during the Engagement phase:

1. Establish and list the facts.

2. Outline and describe the problem.

3. Envision the circumstances of the problem.

Note: Evaluation rubrics, as well as comparison benchmarks, should be designed, articulated, and modeled prior to the Engagement stage. An evaluation rubric is a scoring guide used to evaluate a performance task; it includes specific descriptors of what a particular performance looks like at several different quality levels. A comparison benchmark refers to the use of exemplars (examples chosen to highlight the characteristics of the particular level for which they have been chosen) to establish how different performance levels look. (See Chapter 5 for more information on evaluation.)

Exploration

In the Exploration stage, students have the opportunity to get directly involved with the research and the materials. As they work together in teams, students begin to build a base of common experiences, which in turn assists them in the process of sharing and communicating. During this phase the teacher becomes the facilitator by providing materials and guiding the students' focus. The students' inquiry process is what drives the instruction during the investigation or exploration. Internet research inquiries, field investigations, and team projects are ideal environments for guided inquiry and discovery. During this phase, the teacher is present for support if needed, but encourages students to conduct research, reflect, discuss with their peers, and draw their own conclusions.

Students take part in the following steps in the Exploration process:

1. Organize and analyze the information.

2. Look for patterns and connections.

3. Examine and evaluate facts using critical thinking skills.

4. Make a chart, table, graph, drawing, or model.

5. Select a strategy.
   - Work backward
   - Guess and test
   - Simulate or experiment
   - Make organized list
   - Use logic and deduction
   - Divide into smaller parts
   - Use algebraic or geometric skills
   - Use a calculator

Explanation

The third stage, Explanation, is the point at which the learner begins to put the abstract experience he or she has had into a communicable form. Language helps learners sequence events into a logical format. Communication occurs between peers, the facilitator, or within the learners themselves. Working in groups, learners support each other's understandings as they articulate their observations, ideas, questions, and hypotheses. The facilitator determines levels of understanding and possible misconceptions. Created works such as writings, drawings, videos, or tape recordings are communications that provide recorded evidence of the learner's development, progress, and growth. The teacher's role during this process, as before, is simply to be available to advise the students when they reach a roadblock.

Students take part in the following steps during the Explanation phase of the project:

1. Articulate observations, ideas, questions, and hypotheses.

2. Reflect and write on:
    *   Observations and hypotheses offered
    *   Questions posed and answered

Elaboration

In the fourth stage, Elaboration, students expand on the concepts they have learned, make connections to other related concepts, and apply their understandings to the world around them. Teachers can help students develop alternative solutions by giving an example of two different solutions to the same problem. For example, while researching different departure and arrival times involved in plane travel, a learner constructs an understanding of the concept of different time zones around the world and how time is calculated. Applications and connections to real-world events and circumstances, such as the International Date Line or daylight saving time, often lead to further inquiry and new understandings. Elaborations encourage students to apply or extend their understanding to new but similar situations so they become confident in their newfound knowledge. Additional practice problems, demonstrations, and so forth serve as formative evaluation and feedback mechanisms.

Students engage in the following steps during the Elaboration process:

1. Develop alternative solutions.

2. Make a generalization or develop a new concept from the work.

3. Create variations on the original problem.

Evaluation

Evaluation, the fifth stage, is an ongoing diagnostic process that allows teachers to determine whether learners have attained understanding of concepts and knowledge. Evaluation and assessment can occur at any and all points along the continuum of the instructional process. During both the Engagement and Exploration phases, evaluation should be ongoing, based on teacher observation. In this way, teachers can step in to give feedback before students wander too far off course. The Explanation phase is where learners begin to put abstract experience into communicable forms. Teachers can determine levels of understanding and possible misconceptions by examining student-created works such as writings, drawings, and video or tape recordings. The Elaboration process is where students are encouraged to apply or extend their understandings to new but similar situations so they become confident in their newfound knowledge. At this point, additional practice problems, demonstrations, and so forth serve as formative evaluation and feedback devices, allowing teachers to evaluate through observation and adjust instruction to provide students with what they need. Some of the tools that assist in this diagnostic process are rubrics (quantified and prioritized outcome expectations) designed for the unit (see Chapter 5 for rubrics that can be used for evaluation), teacher observation structured by checklists, student interviews, portfolios designed with specific purposes, project- and PBL products, and embedded assessments.

Students should follow these steps during the Evaluation process:

1. Revisit the rubric and comparison benchmarks.

2. Maintain ongoing communication and feedback with group members as well as with the teacher.

The Role of Evaluation in Constructivist Learning

Evaluation is a very important component of constructivist learning, as concrete evidence of the learning process allows for valuable communication between students, teachers, parents, and administrators. Progress displays, which are the practice of collecting student work from different stages of growth to establish a pattern of learning progress, can be used to enhance understanding for all parties involved in the educational process. These can also become starting points for further enrichment of the student's education. This type of evidence is what guides the teacher in further lesson planning and may even signal the need for modification and change of direction. For example, if teachers find evidence of confusion or misconception, they can revisit a concept to further clarify understanding. If students show profound interest in a divergent direction of inquiry, teachers can consider refocusing the investigation to take advantage of the high interest level.

Constructivist philosophy views the evaluation process as continuous, with learning being open ended and open to change. An ongoing loop exists where questions lead not only to answers, but also to more questions, and instruction is driven by both predetermined lesson design and the inquiry process.

Learning something new, or attempting to understand something familiar in greater depth, is not a linear process. In trying to make sense of a new concept or idea, individuals use both their prior experience and the firsthand knowledge gained from new inquiry explorations. Initially, curiosity about a topic is stirred when individuals are stimulated by something intriguing. Then individuals poke, probe, inquire about, and explore this idea until it becomes less mysterious. As individuals begin to investigate new ideas, they put together bits and pieces of prior explorations that seem to fit their understandings of the invention or phenomenon they are investigating. For example, in the case of a roller coaster, individuals may realize that there is an association between speed, velocity, and the circular motion of the roller coaster car that results in centrifugal force. In

PBL, evaluation takes the form of individuals sharing their learning process and how they arrived at a solution. Individuals also share how they can apply what they learned to other situations and experiences.

TEACHING IN THE PROBLEM-BASED LEARNING CLASSROOM

In a traditional classroom the teacher disseminates knowledge either through direct instruction or by spoon-feeding students isolated facts and pieces of information. In such a classroom it is likely that students do written work in the form of workbooks or worksheets. In a PBL, brain-compatible classroom, instruction and assessment utilize a multiple intelligences approach. Students are provided with a wide variety of topics, instructional methods, and presentation and assessment styles that enable them to construct their own meaningful learning and encourage the evolution of sophisticated understandings. To achieve this greater comprehension, students need opportunities to discuss and debate unfamiliar concepts and ideas. They need to be able to test their understandings and participate in the higher-level thinking that accompanies such active dialogue. It is through such discussion and debate that shared meanings are developed and advanced and meaningful learning is personalized.

Teachers can use many methods to foster discussion and debate in their classrooms. Several of these are outlined in Figure 2.1.

Without participatory dialogue, learning remains removed from an individual's experiences and mental connections. Learning that takes place without personal connections is elusive and difficult to retain.

When students are active rather than passive learners, they are better able to process and integrate new information. Inquiry methods of teaching are student centered rather than teacher centered, and problem based rather than solution based. Thus, the kind of learning that occurs is active rather than

Figure 2.1   Ten Methods for Initiating Discussion and Dialogue

Teachers can:

1. Provide opportunities for hands-on learning
2. Ask open-ended, inquiry questions
3. Encourage students to ask questions
4. Encourage students to initiate ideas
5. Encourage students to investigate their own ideas and questions
6. Encourage students to discuss and challenge each other's ideas and conceptualizations
7. Use student questions and responses to develop topics that are relevant and meaningful
8. Encourage the use of multiple information sources rather than just one text
9. Encourage student reflection
10. Avoid supplying answers or explanations

Figure 2.2   Comparison of Student-Centered and Teacher-Centered Methods

---

INDUCTIVE METHODS (STUDENT CENTERED)

TEACHER:
Here are some data. What questions do these data create in your mind?

DEDUCTIVE METHODS (TEACHER CENTERED)

TEACHER:
Here is the rule. Here are some examples. Do them to refine your understanding of the rule.

---

passive. Figure 2.2 shows an example of student-centered teaching methods as compared to teacher-centered teaching methods.

The centerpiece of the PBL approach to instruction is the inadequately structured or incomplete problem. By working to solve authentic problems, students assume the roles of working professionals. They readily take responsibility for their own learning because they are truly excited about and engaged in the work at hand.

PBL problems include only enough information to suggest how the learner might proceed with the inquiry, but never enough information to enable him or her to solve the problem without further investigation. Formulas alone are not enough to solve these open-ended problems; students must apply their critical thinking skills. PBL enables students to evolve into problem solvers by honing the skills of reasoning, collaboration, and persistence.

The success of PBL in professional fields has proven irresistible to educators who are interested in instructional methods that fuel students' enthusiasm for learning. The PBL model has been used in fields such as medical education, as interns and residents do rounds with established doctors and make diagnoses for illnesses. It has also been successful in other professions, such as aviation, where student pilots are presented with various problem situations regarding flight and are asked to reach an appropriate solution.

Innovators of the past such as Euclid, Archimedes, Galileo, and Newton wrote about particular problems that sparked their special interests. PBL is a methodology that can ignite that kind of spark in today's students. When students are given inadequately constructed problems to solve, they learn to think the way real-world professionals such as architects, archaeologists, engineers, scientists, and historians think. Such thinking requires that students first analyze the problem to determine which pieces of the puzzle are missing (for example, which learning issues are missing). PBL teaches students that they must first discern exactly what the problem is instead of immediately jumping to the solution. To find the real problem, students must identify what they already know about it by constructing hypotheses based upon prior knowledge. They can then identify the learning issues involved, decide what new information is needed, and determine how they must test this new information to refine their original theories. Only after taking the problem through this process are students able to proceed to a solution. Teachers can use Figure 2.3, the Solution Path Outline, with their students to help them follow this path. This graphic organizer can be used to help students organize

Figure 2.3   Solution Path Outline

1. Restate the problem in your own words:

    • What specific information is given?

    _____

    _____

    • What do I already know about this problem?

    _____

    _____

2. Form the hypothesis:

    • What am I looking for?

    _____

    _____

    • How can I get to the answer?

    _____

    _____

3. Identify learning issues:

    • Exactly what information do I need to learn to obtain an appropriate answer?

    _____

    _____

4. Research learning issues:

    • What new information could I learn concerning these issues and where would I find this information?

    _____

    _____

5. Test new information:

    • Does this new information bring me closer to a resolution?

    _____

    _____

    • Is it a correct and accurate resolution?

    _____

    _____

    • Does the information enable me to refine my original theories?

    _____

    _____

    • Will the information help me find an appropriate answer?

    _____

    _____

6. Proceed to resolution/solution.

their thoughts and learn the steps involved in the problem-solving process. By using the Solution Path Outline at the beginning of each PBL unit, students develop the habits and skills needed to become good problem solvers. Each student team should use the organizer during the discussion process, which is where much of the learning takes place.

Many teachers may embrace PBL in theory but shy away from actively using the approach in the classroom, since crafting open and messy problems can be a time-consuming challenge. Teachers also have to be willing to let their students take the lead, relinquish control, and act as the coach or guide instead of the leader.

Since many experienced teachers who are using PBL for the first time may fear that it may be difficult to work with, it is a good idea for teachers to begin using PBL on a small scale. Teachers can either start with a single problem that can be easily integrated into the existing curriculum or devise a way to teach the existing curriculum in a problem-based manner. Teachers can begin locating problems by looking through textbooks, curriculum guides, newspapers, and magazines to find situations, dilemmas, and issues that need resolution.

Structuring the Messy Problem

Problems can be structured around many subjects. For example, problem solving is a part of creating art, because when an artist makes a decision about how to paint a landscape, she is, in fact, problem solving. She has to decide what colors to use, and she conducts experiments to determine what blend of colors will result in the desired shade. She has to think about the use of perspective as well as positive and negative space. In essence, she is behaving like a scientist by solving problems before creating her art.

In addition to being inherent in tasks, problems can also be structured around current events to link real life with learning objectives. In fact, one of the best ways teachers can bring problem solving closer to home is by using local newspapers as a resource for new and unique problem situations. The most meaningful and relevant problems for students are those that affect them directly. For example, if the local community is in need of a new playground, teachers might ask students to put together a plan and a design for such a playground. Putting together the plan would engage students' problem solving, computation and estimation, measurement, telecommunications, and researching skills.

The following is an example of an authentic, real-life problem that might occur in a community.

Situation: A town is currently in the midst of planning construction for a new recreation area that is surrounded by water. The town must first find a practical way of getting machinery, supplies, and employees to the designated construction site.

This situation is ripe with problem-solving possibilities. Teachers could ask students to design plans for alternative ways to connect the recreation site to the main roads. The students' challenge might first be to devise answers for the following questions: What different bridge designs could be used? What size weight load does the bridge need to be rated for? What other methods for connection might be considered? What sort of construction costs would such projects entail? This project could even be extended to help students use what they have learned to solve similar problems related to other curricula. Once teachers become comfortable delivering curriculum through a problem-based approach, it becomes much easier to create open-ended, messy problems that are also interdisciplinary.

An instructional environment that is most conducive to successful problem solving and inquiry techniques possesses the following:

- A group learning situation
- Unfamiliar subject matter that results in challenging but solvable problems
- Available resources students can use to find answers (the students must already possess the skills necessary to use these resources)
- Students with the ability to "think for themselves," feel strongly about the subject matter, and learn from "real" situations or examples
- Flexible time allotment

For PBL to be truly meaningful, students must learn to grapple with more than one problem a semester or a term, as the repeated use of problem-solving skills encourages the greatest metacognitive gains. However, the way curriculum is currently organized must change so that there is a place in the curriculum for inquiry and PBL. Fewer topics should be covered during the school year, and those topics should be covered in greater depth. (This is one of the main recommendations from the National Center for Education Statistics Third International Mathematics and Science Study conducted in 1998.) The only way to include PBL in a curriculum that insists on remaining "a mile wide and an inch deep" (Schmidt, 1996) is to begin on a small scale, with one PBL unit a year. By substituting one of the units in this book for a text chapter that covers similar material, the related text chapter can be shortened or even eliminated. Each year teachers can include another PBL unit in lieu of a traditional text chapter until they have a repertoire of PBL units that cover the same material as the text, but in a much more relevant and meaningful manner. When PBL is linked to standards and high-quality content, high-quality learning, increased student enthusiasm, excitement, and curiosity result.

In order to teach PBL effectively, teachers need to develop several personal characteristics. Teachers need to become amenable to relinquishing absolute power and control over classroom proceedings. During PBL, it is acceptable for teachers to say, "I don't know the answer to that question, but let's find out." If teachers provide students with all the information or answers during a PBL activity, they are hindering the students' learning. This idea is supported by neuroscientific and cognitive research that indicates that active engagement on the part of the learner is necessary for enduring learning to occur. According to the National Research Council (2000), "Neuroscientific research confirms the important role that experience plays in building the structure of the mind by modifying structures in the brain" (p. 25). Learning is the active process through which an individual's experiences provide the basis for his or her understandings. Thus, teachers who aren't naturally inclined to be coaches will have to take a leap of faith and trust that this role provides the greatest benefit to their students.

Giving students opportunities for hands-on learning, allowing them to apply their previous knowledge to an activity, and allowing them to lead their learning results in students who understand and retain more about what they learn. Students are given opportunities to engage in these types of learning in the following integrated inquiry project.

INTEGRATED INQUIRY PROJECT: MIDDLE/ SECONDARY LEVEL: DEVELOPING ENTREPRENEURIAL EXCELLENCE

The following project has been designed for middle- to secondary-level students. It presents a project unit based on the real-world integration of mathematics, science, and technology. The premise of this project unit is that student teams are to have the experience of designing and developing original and viable business plans. Project instructions lead students from the initial step of brainstorming ideas for potential businesses right through the presentation of the business plan to potential financial backers.

A cost estimation plan and a worksheet have been provided to help students with organizing data.

Project Standards (Grades 6–8)

I. Mathematics Content Standards (Adapted From the National Council of Teachers of Mathematics, 2000)

Standard 1: Numbers and Operations

Instructional programs from pre-kindergarten through grade 12 should enable all students to

- Understand numbers, ways of representing numbers, relationships among numbers, and number systems
- Understand the meaning of operations and how they relate to one another
- Compute fluently and make reasonable estimates

Standard 3: Geometry

Instructional programs from pre-kindergarten through grade 12 should enable all students to

- Use visualization, spatial reasoning, and geometric modeling to solve problems

Standard 4: Measurement

Instructional programs from pre-kindergarten through grade 12 should enable all students to

- Understand attributes, units, and systems of measurement
- Apply a variety of techniques, tools, and formulas for determining measurements

Standard 5: Data Analysis and Probability

Instructional programs from pre-kindergarten through grade 12 should enable all students to

- Develop and evaluate inferences and predictions that are based on data

Standard 6: Problem Solving

Instructional programs from pre-kindergarten through grade 12 should enable all students to

- Build new mathematical knowledge through problem solving
- Solve problems that arise in mathematics and in other contexts
- Apply and adopt a wide variety of strategies to solve problems
- Monitor and reflect on the process of mathematical problem solving

Standard 7: Reasoning and Proof

Instructional programs from pre-kindergarten through grade 12 should enable all students to

- Select and use various types of reasoning and methods of proof

Standard 8: Communication

Instructional programs from pre-kindergarten through grade 12 should enable all students to

- Organize and consolidate their mathematical thinking through communication
- Analyze and evaluate the mathematical thinking and strategies of others

Standard 9: Connections

Instructional programs from pre-kindergarten through grade 12 should enable all students to

- Recognize and apply mathematics in contexts outside of mathematics

Standard 10: Representation

Instructional programs from pre-kindergarten through grade 12 should enable all students to

- Create and use representations to organize, record, and communicate mathematical ideas
- Select, apply, and translate among mathematical representations to solve problems

II. Science Content Standards (Adapted From the *National Science Education Standards*, 1995)

Content Standard A: Science as Inquiry

Students should develop:
- Abilities necessary to do scientific inquiry
- Understandings about scientific inquiry

Content Standard E: Science and Technology

Students should develop:

- Abilities of technological design
- Understandings about science and technology

Content Standard F: Science in Personal and Social Perspectives

Students should develop an understanding of:

- Populations, resources, and environments
- Natural hazards
- Science and technology in society

III. Technology Foundation Standards (International Society for Technology in Education [ISTE]) (Adapted From the *National Educational Technology Standards [NETS] Project*, 1998)

Basic Operations and Concepts

- Students demonstrate a sound understanding of the nature and operation of technology systems.
- Students are proficient in the use of technology.

Social, Ethical, and Human Issues

- Students understand the ethical, cultural, and societal issues related to technology.
- Students practice responsible use of technology systems, information, and software.
- Students develop positive attitudes toward technology uses that support lifelong learning, collaboration, personal pursuits, and productivity.

Technology Productivity Tools

- Students use technology tools to enhance learning, increase productivity, and promote creativity.
- Students use productivity tools to collaborate in constructing technology-enhanced models, preparing publications, and producing other creative works.

Technology Communications Tools

- Students use telecommunications to collaborate, publish, and interact with peers, experts, and other audiences.
- Students use a variety of media and formats to communicate information and ideas effectively to multiple audiences.

Technology Research Tools

- Students use technology to locate, evaluate, and collect information from a variety of sources.
- Students use technology tools to process data and report results.

- Students evaluate and select new information resources and technological innovations based on the appropriateness to specific tasks.

Technology Problem-Solving and Decision-Making Tools

- Students use technology resources for solving problems and making informed decisions.
- Students employ technology in the development of strategies for solving problems in the real world.

Performance Task

Student teams are to develop an economic good or service around which a small business partnership can be formed. Students are to work in pairs, and using the Internet as a resource guide, design and/or construct a machine, a process, or a theory that will improve an aspect of life today.

Each team must compose and present their business plan to the board of directors (rest of the class) and convince them that the new business is a worthwhile loan risk as well as an asset to the chosen area of establishment (park, mall, neighborhood, and so forth).

Project Instructions

The project instructions (see Figure 2.4) should be given to students as a handout and then discussed by individual teams before the teacher goes over

Figure 2.4   Project Instructions for Developing a Business Plan

---

STEP 1: START WITH AN IDEA

Brainstorm the kinds of goods or services you might use for a business. Then, design a new product or modify something that already exists. Once your plan is formulated, your team must submit it in writing in 50 words or less.

STEP 2: RESEARCH

Some important questions your team might keep in mind when forming business ideas include:

- How will you know whether the product or design is feasible?
- How will you know if it works?
- How will you know whether or not consumers will want it?
- What kinds of tests, tools, or instruments (e.g., surveys) will you use to research such questions?

Once the preliminary research has been conducted, your team should evaluate their results and make any necessary modifications. (Some ideas may need to be changed if potential consumers are not excited about the original idea.) Results to be handed in include design tests, design analyses, surveys, and survey analyses.

STEP 3: BUSINESS PLAN

Your teams should put together a business plan. The purpose of the business plan is to help your team organize their thoughts and ideas for the business aspect of the unit. The plan will also help your team determine what resources you will need to carry the plan to fruition. Business plans are very important when seeking financial backing for any new product or idea.

Figure 2.5   Creating a Business Plan

Follow the steps listed and answer the questions to create a successful business plan.

1. Create a cover page and table of contents for your team's plan.
2. Include a business description of your team's plan.

To create a complete business description, first describe the company. Start out by asking, Who are the company's founders? Briefly describe the people who will run the company. Include their backgrounds and qualifications. How active will the founders be in the business?

Next, explain the basic business idea. This explanation should include a detailed description of the goods or services to be provided. Be sure to emphasize what is unique about the product or service. Describe how the business will fit into its surroundings. Explain how it will benefit the immediate area or neighborhood.

3. Include a list of productive resources needed for the business in your plan.

The list of productive resources should cover the following areas:

   a. Land: What natural resources will be needed?
   b. Labor: How many and what kind of employees will be needed? What sort of work will they be performing? What will their pay be? What benefits (vacation, medical coverage, and so forth) will they receive?
   c. Capital: How will the money to finance the company be raised? What sort of equipment does the business require? What will the facility (plant) look like?
   d. Management: How will the business be managed?

4. Each plan should include information regarding who the customers will be.

Your team should ask, What group of customers will be interested in our group's product or service? Be thorough and specific when describing the potential customers you plan to target. What are the characteristics of this target audience? What is the particular age group of your customers? How can your target group be differentiated from others?

5. Include knowledge regarding your competition.

Your team should ask, With whom in the area will you be competing for these customers' dollars? If the customers don't spend money at your business, where would they spend it? Answering this question demonstrates that you understand your competition and proves you understand the industry you hope to enter. Explain why your competitors don't meet consumers' needs as well as your business will. Discuss why you will be able to capture a share of this market.

6. Include information on pricing.

Entrepreneurs will not produce if the costs of production and profit making are not covered. Your team should ask, How much will it cost to produce your product or service? How many units of your product or service can realistically be produced in a year, and in a month? What will you charge for your product or service?
Complete the Cost Estimate Plan worksheet. This will help you with both pricing and financing.
Once the above information is complete, your team is ready to put together your plan presentation.

the assignment with the entire class. Figure 2.5 should also be given to students to use as guidelines for creating their business plans. Students can use the Cost Estimate Plan worksheet (see Figure 2.6) to consider expenses. This worksheet can be kept more open ended for advanced students, thereby allowing them to research competitive interest rates and/or other loan calculations.

Figure 2.6   Cost Estimate Plan

Use the following worksheet to complete your cost estimate plan.

Cost Estimating Worksheet

Business Name:_____

Entrepreneurs: _____

_____

A. Fixed Expenses		B. Variable Costs	
Rent	$ _____	Raw materials/merchandise	
Renovation and/or		_____	$ _____
construction	$ _____	_____	$ _____
Equipment	$ _____	_____	$ _____
License(s)	$ _____	_____	$ _____
Transportation	$ _____	_____	$ _____
Uniforms	$ _____	Power (electricity and fuel)	$ _____
Insurance	$ _____	Wages	$ _____
Other	$ _____	Advertising	$ _____
Other	$ _____	Other?	$ _____
Total A	$ _____	Total C	$ _____

C. Loan/Capital Cost		D.	
Total A × 0.75 =	$ _____ (1)	D. Total Cost Per Month Using a calculator, find the number of items and the selling price of each so as to be certain your team's enterprise will be viable and profitable.	$ _____
Loan (1) × 0.11 =	$ _____ (2)		
Interest per year (2) × 6 =	$ _____ (3)		
Loan (1) + total interest (3) =	$ _____ (4)		
Total amount owed bank (4) divided by 72 =	$ _____ (5)	Minimum to sell	$ _____
This is the fixed amount you must pay the bank each month.		Price per unit	$ _____

1.   Use the fixed cost items (Section A) to estimate the cost of some of the basics your business will need to pay for. These costs (fixed expenses) must be covered, even if nothing is sold. Note: Not every business will require all the listed items. Therefore, adjust accordingly. Use your best estimate of the total cost of these items to determine your start-up costs. Add all these items to get Total A.

2.   After you have added up your fixed expenses (Total A), you can determine the amount that must be borrowed from the bank and the interest on that amount (see Section B). You will need to take a bank loan for 75 percent of Total A for a minimum of six years at the prime lending rate plus two (that is, if the prime lending rate is 9 percent you will pay 11 percent interest). You will be given a six-year loan. Therefore, you must pay back 1/72 of the total loan plus interest each month. You need to determine your total capital outlay per month. This can be calculated by:
   * Multiplying Total A times 0.75 to find out what your basic loan will be.
   * Multiplying the amount of your basic loan by .11 to determine your yearly interest.
   * Multiplying your interest by 6 since you must pay the interest for six years (I = PRT).
   * Adding your basic loan to your total interest for six years. This will give you a grand total of what you'll have to pay the bank.
   * Dividing your grand total by 72 to calculate the amount you must pay the bank each month.

3.   Go to Section B, Variable Costs. These numbers may vary from month to month, depending on your sales. Use this to estimate your monthly operating costs. When you are finished, total your monthly operating costs to get Total C.
   Add your total variable costs per month (Total C) to the amount you need to pay the bank each month (amount at bottom of Section C). This will give you a total cost per month (Total D).

4.   Questions to ponder:
   * How much will you have to sell of your goods or services each month in order to break even and cover your costs?
   * What is a reasonable number of items or units of service that you can make and sell in a month?
   * How much will you have to sell your items or services for to cover your total monthly costs?

(Continued)

Figure 2.6 (Continued)

When you have achieved a number that
- Will cover your expenses
- Will give you some profit
- Is within your ability in time and effort, and
- Will get you customers

you are in business.

Resources

Students can use the following Web sites for research.

www.bplans.com/

This Web site offers sample business plans that were selected because they have already been approved for funding, or simply represent a quality business plan. The site directs users to free interactive tools that can help potential entrepreneurs figure out when they will break even or the potential a proposed business may have. The Plan Wizard, also at this site, asks users simple questions to match their business plan to their specific business needs.

www.smallbusinessbc.ca/

www.smallbusinessbc.ca/index.php

This is a Web site of the Canada/British Columbia Business Service Centre set up for small businesses. It contains links for online small business workshops, company export/import directories, market information, an interactive business planner, and more.

www.kidsway.com

This Web site calls itself "America's leading provider of business, entrepreneurship, career, and investment education for youth ages 8–19."

www.youngandsuccessful.com

This "Young Entrepreneurs' Network" provides a forum for questions regarding various aspects of business development.

http://www.eventuring.org/eShip/appmanager/eVenturing/eVenturingDesktop

This Web site contains world resources for entrepreneurs, including articles, newsletters, and a business assistance network.

Presentation

The final phase of this project is the presentation. Teachers should share the following information with students.

Each business has to be accepted by the board of directors (the class) before your team can start earning a profit. Convince them to take a chance on investing in your enterprise. This presentation should make use of the available technological resources as creatively as possible. For example, each team could design a PowerPoint presentation as well as a model of the product. (There are many other options for using technological resources to create a presentation. Be creative!)

Aspects and Approaches of Problem-Based Learning

For many educators schooled in traditional K–12 teaching methods, implementing problem-based learning (PBL) may at times seem overwhelming. In the PBL process, teachers need to help learners build their own problem-solving skills and thinking abilities while teaching the content necessary to apply those skills. The fact of the matter, however, is that when the PBL process is broken down into steps, it can be easily applied to everyday teaching situations. More than eight decades after the following quote by John Dewey (1944/1916) was written, students still learn best by thinking through and by engaging in problems.

> Methods which are permanently successful in formal education go back to the type of situation which causes reflection out of school and in ordinary life. They give pupils something to do, not something to learn; and the doing is of such a nature as to demand thinking, or the intention of noting connections; learning naturally results. (p. 154)

PHASES OF IMPLEMENTATION

PBL operates best when approached in three distinct phases:

1. Problem design

2. Locating and identifying resources

3. Problem analysis

Teachers should approach these phases by first making all problem design decisions and then integrating the three components into a coherent whole. The entire problem plan must be well thought out prior to being presented to students.

Problem Design

In the first phase, the problem design phase, the problem may be voiced as a question, a case study, an example, a charge, a hypothesis, or a situation. The problem should be realistic, so that students can relate to its context. While the problem statement itself may not contain all the necessary information, it must not be ambiguous. In addition, the requirements for solving the problem must be clearly stated in comprehensible language. The problem should be solvable, and sufficient resources should be offered to provide for multiple answers and solutions.

Locating and Identifying Resources

The second phase, the resource phase, refers to the stage when students gather data as well as acquire learning resources and engage in experiences. Teachers can introduce students to several different forms of resources:

- *Direct experiences* refer to making or creating things, working in a real work situation, going to a concert or play, or designing something. For example, teachers could engage students in a direct experience by asking them to construct a bridge model.
- *Contrived direct experiences* most often involve field trips, visiting sites, or listening to speakers. Teachers could engage students in a contrived direct experience by taking them to bridge sites and asking them to note how the construction was done.
- *Dramatic participation* refers to role plays and/or simulation games. This applies to the type of problem-solving experience demonstrated when students take on the roles of professionals in real-world jobs.
- *Demonstrations* can comprise observing experts, working models, and/or the application and utilization of technology. For example, teachers could use demonstration as a resource by asking students to use a software program that deals with aspects of construction such as transfer of weight or suspension.
- *Exhibits* denote viewing artifacts or static displays of technology, such as a visit to an actual bridge constructed in the same manner as the model being created by students.

- *Visual and aural materials* most often consist of charts, graphs, statistical data displays, photographs, videotapes, or CD-ROM disks.
- *Written materials* consist of books, articles, computer programs, poetry, and/or manuals of construction.

All of these are suitable resources for the PBL experience and can be used alone or in combination. For example, if a teacher gave students the problem of finding ways to reduce traffic jams in their town, he or she might want students to attend a lecture by someone who has studied traffic patterns (contrived direct experiences) in addition to providing students with data on current traffic statistics (visual and aural materials). When choosing which resource or combination of resources to introduce to students for a particular problem, teachers should consider factors such as the age of the students, their mobility and ease of travel, and their levels of sophistication and independence.

Teachers also need to keep in mind that good resources are relevant to the problem; develop the inquiry skills of thinking, researching, and problem solving; are accurate, valid, and up to date; and help develop the students' sense of discovery. Teachers should make resources available for use within set time frames (keeping in mind the need for flexibility in first-time PBL projects) and should make sure the chosen resources allow for a variety of learning approaches and styles. Most important, teachers need to determine that the resources offered support the development of student problem-solving skills. Such resources encourage original thinking and creativity, engender discussion, and give rise to reflection. Using authentic, primary sources of information (such as well-known Web sites rather than textbooks), students can become familiar with the type of information professionals use in their daily work.

Problem Analysis

In the final phase of PBL, the problem analysis phase, the teacher's role is to encourage students to offer answers, hypotheses, and reflections that may consist of either closed or open inquiries. Closed inquiries have definite answers, while open and active inquiries may have answers but more often have conclusions based on analysis and reflection. Opportunities for processing, analyzing, reflecting, and engaging in other metacognitive activities are vital to students' ability to reach valid conclusions (Ronis, 2006). Teachers can encourage students to engage in such activities through group and individual reflections.

PROBLEM-BASED LEARNING TECHNIQUES

PBL techniques are methods teachers can use to initiate a PBL experience. These techniques come in various forms, such as the inquiry contract, the case study, simulations, workshops, and study questions. Teachers can use these techniques when presenting their students with a messy problem.

The Inquiry Contract

One method teachers can use to facilitate PBL is the *inquiry contract*. For this method, inquiry problems are stated as an inquiry question or a hypothesis. Then, students sign an inquiry contract, which specifies the required outcome and the process that should be used to achieve it, in effect agreeing to complete the project in a manner consistent with high standards. An inquiry contract may be negotiated with a group or individuals. It may require practical research and exploration; it may extend over several lessons or be contained in a single lesson.

With an inquiry contract, it is the facilitator's job to

- Clearly define the research question or help students define the question
- Negotiate a process that can be completed on time and for which resources are available
- Ascertain that students have the required skills to answer the question
- Set success criteria or negotiate these criteria with the students
- Check on student progress by establishing a timetable with regular meetings
- Be aware of students who might be experiencing difficulties and provide them with help
- Evaluate the contract according to the established success criteria

Inquiry contracts, whether for a group or an individual learning project, should always provide specific information. Essentially, these are contracts in which teachers define what they expect students to do in the project. The students demonstrate their willingness to adhere to the expectations for the project by signing the contract.

Figure 3.1 shows an inquiry contract that has been prepared for elementary-level students. Teachers can review this contract to determine what information they need to give to their students. Teachers can also use the PBL project described in the figure as a project to do with their own students. A blank Inquiry Contract is provided in Figure 3.2 for teachers to use with their own students and problem projects or units.

Case Studies: Open or Closed

A *case study* is usually a comprehensive oral, written, and/or filmed account of a real event (or a series of related events), in which the problem to be solved is established. The case may be teacher centered, meaning the problem is solved through questions and answers; student centered, meaning a student works alone to analyze and solve the problem; or group centered, where a group of students analyze and solve the problem together (see the multilevel Internet project in Chapter 4).

It is the teacher/facilitator's job to construct the case study to include each of the following elements:

- A detailed incident
- A well-sequenced set of events

Figure 3.1   Sample Inquiry Contract

Names: Bobby Smith, Jimmy Thomas, Fatima Right, and Susan Jones

Date: March 12, 2006

Course: Math   Topic: Money, finance, and budget planning

Timetable: 1 week

Initial meeting to negotiate contract:

Team C consisting of Bobby, Jimmy, Fatima, and Susan will first plan a budget outlining the way they will spend their team portion of the total party budget. Next, they will work out the details as to what they will need in the way of party supplies. To help them plan what kind of foods and party items to purchase, the four teams will take a trip to a local market where they can do their research. This research will provide the data the team needs to make a budget chart for their portion of the unit. The report will be presented to the class before the party on Friday.

Intermediate progress check:

Fatima and Susan have done most of the planning for what kind of salty snacks to buy, but all four of the students were productive comparison shoppers in our initial trip to the store.

Final hand-in deadline:

All written plans, budget charts, and receipts are to be handed in by Friday before the party.

Learning objectives:

Mathematics

- To explore the concept of money and how finances work
- To develop the concept of equivalency, both kinesthetically and conceptually
- To use basic procedures while performing the process of computation
- To understand and apply basic properties of the concepts of measurement
- To effectively use a variety of strategies in the problem-solving process
- To develop group problem-solving skills and team dynamics

Technology

- To use calculators and computers effectively
- To use the Internet as a research source
- To understand the nature of technological design
- To understand the interactions of math, technology, and society

Processes to be followed:

Students are to work in teams of four for the project. Each of the four class teams is responsible for one of the four necessary party categories. Team A is in charge of drinks and beverages; Team B decides what kind and color of paper goods will be used at the party; Team C chooses the salty snack foods; and Team D is in charge of the sweets. To help them plan what kind of foods and party items to purchase, the four teams will take a trip to a local market where they can do their "research" as a team. This research consists of identifying and comparing different items and brands. The teams will need to keep track of the different items, as well as the cost of each item for the data analysis project component back in the classroom. The team will then make a budget chart poster for their portion of the unit, which they will present to the class before the party on Friday. The teams are now ready to plan their purchases based on how much money they have in the team budget for their part of "Project: Party!" (At this point, some teacher and team consultation will be scheduled so that each team can get feedback as to whether or not they are being reasonable in their budget and choices.) Then, the agreed-upon amount of money is collected within the teams; each team coordinator is in charge of collecting that group's money. The recorder keeps a list of who brought in what amount, and both the resource person and the materials manager have the job of making sure the correct amount has been collected and credited. The class teams will make the actual "purchasing" trip to the store, but this time each team has a specific list of supplies to buy along with the anticipated cost of each item. The reward for all their hard work will be the class party.

Learning resources to be used:

- Materials for budget poster: Colored construction paper, scissors, glue, colored pencils, and markers
- Materials for research: Calculators and advertisement section from newspaper with local food prices
- Students can research food prices on the Internet to do comparison shopping.

Criteria for success:

- The team supplies their portion of the party refreshments and stays within their budget.
- Budget poster is legible, easy to understand, and makes sense to the other students.
- Evidence to be presented:
  - Completed budget poster

Figure 3.2   Blank Inquiry Contract

Name(s): _____   Date: _____

Course: _____   Topic: _____

Timetable:

    Initial meeting to negotiate contract: _____

    Intermediate progress check: _____

    Final hand-in deadline: _____

Learning objectives (intended learning outcomes): _____

_____

_____

_____

Processes to be followed: _____

_____

_____

_____

Learning resources to be used: _____

_____

_____

_____

Criteria for success: _____

_____

_____

_____

Evidence to be presented: _____

_____

_____

_____

- Statements of fact based on sound research
- A problem to be addressed

The teacher should clearly state the purposes of the case study and set a time limit for finding a solution. In a teacher-centered case study, the teacher is involved throughout. In a student- or group-centered case study, the students are encouraged to reach their own conclusions, but the teacher remains available to clarify issues, provide feedback, and arbitrate technical issues. At the end of the case study the teacher reviews the results for evaluation. Figure 3.3 offers an example of a group-centered case study that can be used as a problem-based learning experience.

Figure 3.3   Group-Centered Case Study

Case: Jim and Kathy Robbins are meeting with your group, Financial Advisors, Inc., for some advice on a financial matter. They have accumulated $17,503 of credit card debt that spins off a monthly interest charge based on an annual rate of 18%, and they are starting to feel the pressures of the interest charges. Jim expects to inherit some money in the future, but this may not happen for a long time.

Jim and Kathy really need to pay off this debt so that they can start to save for their children's college education. They want to begin paying the debt but are not sure how to begin.

Current financial situation:
Jim, a teacher, earns $46,200 a year before taxes.
Kathy, a secretary, earns $396 a week after taxes.
Their fixed expenses are

- Mortgage payment: $1,485 per month
- Utilities and phone: $270 per month
- Car payment: $346 per month

Past financial history: Jim and Kathy have never been in this much debt before. They still owe $2,300 to Jim's cousin, which they are paying at 8% interest per year, and they have tapped out their savings account.

Situation review: Before Jim and Kathy can try to work out a plan for paying this debt, they must try to anticipate any additional expenses they may incur for this year. The market value of their home is $255,000, but they have only paid $50,500 of the principal.

Problem assignment: As the Robbins's financial advisors, what kind of financial plan would you recommend for them? How would you advise them to deal with your recommendations?

Simulations: Open

A *simulation* is a "real-life" situation mirrored in a play with tightly scripted roles. Simulations can be given in written form as well as acted out. The implications of a situation that is acted out should be thoroughly planned and discussed before the simulation so students can get an idea of the goals of the simulation. The simulation may be in the form of "in-basket exercises" (a simulation where students have to sort through whatever information, tasks, jobs, and so on must be carried out by the "main character" for a particular day) or a role play in a simulated situation such as pilot training, chairing a meeting, or being interviewed. Simulations are best suited for learning situations in which role playing can be used to help develop the desired problem-solving skills.

With a simulation it is the teacher/facilitator's job to

- Prepare the situation carefully or use an already published situation
- Clearly state the learning purposes for the simulation
- Establish the simulation context and explain the rules and procedures
- Fill the positions
- Clarify issues, provide feedback, and arbitrate on technical disputes about rules during the simulation
- Review processes, outcomes, and behaviors at the simulation's end
- Evaluate group interactions during the simulation (by observing whether groups are applying the desired problem-solving skills, or whether they need more direction)

Figure 3.4 shows an example of a simulation project teachers can use with students.

Workshops: Open or Closed Action

With *workshops*, students "retreat" from a common workplace (such as the classroom) to solve a problem by sharing experiences or knowledge and conducting research and/or completing tasks. Workshopped problems may be broad and open (developing a plan or course of action) or narrow and closed (fixing a malfunctioning engine). Workshops are beneficial when the group is concentrating on research and planning skills.

With workshopping it is the teacher/facilitator's job to

- Clearly state the purposes of the workshop as well as the problem to be solved
- Be sure students experience the workshop as a group and have the requisite skills to solve the problem
- Assemble all the necessary materials to be used (computers with Internet access, hard copy references, recording material, examples)
- Agree on ground rules about workshop processes
- Be available as a consultant when asked
- Set and monitor time limits
- Debrief the group: "What are your conclusions?" "Why?" "What went well?" "What could you have done differently or better?"
- Make a written record of both the process and the results of the workshop. (Teachers can share this with the class, but it is also helpful for reporting student growth to parents.)

Figures 3.5–3.7 show examples of types of workshops that can be conducted with elementary-, middle-, and secondary-level students, respectively.

Figure 3.4   In-Basket Simulation Project

Your name is Jennifer Johnson, age 38, and you have recently been appointed Project Director for the design of a new communications satellite for a fledgling TV satellite dish company called Stardish, Inc. You have five years of experience working as a physicist for NASA, but have never worked in a director's position.

There are three people on your staff—a junior physicist and two engineers. Like you, they are new to the company and have never designed a TV communications satellite before. Your position is supposed to be administrative, but you can see from the first day that you will have to be a very "hands-on" supervisor.

A financial management board controls the monies for all projects, and you are required to attend all their meetings. You are in charge of all the design and financial planning for the project, which includes product design and execution, budget, cost control, purchasing of equipment/supplies, as well as the supervision of your staff.

Immediate Situation

You have arrived at work at 7:30 a.m. on Tuesday, November 11, after your main design engineer has called in sick for the next three days with the flu. You have estimated it will take you approximately one hour to finish preparing the data required for the finance board meeting later in the morning.

Your in-basket contains the following items and your first task is to sort through them:

- Item 1: A message from your dentist requesting that you change your appointment
- Item 2: A notice from the company bank that the papers for this morning's meeting were sent to the wrong address and have been returned to the bank instead of being sent to your office
- Item 3: A notice from the design team that they can't locate one part of the demonstration kit they need for their presentation to the finance board
- Item 4: A notice from the cafeteria requesting direction on what they will be serving at the morning meeting
- Item 5: A notice of a meeting with the finance board at 11 a.m.

Doing the In-Basket

On a sheet of paper, list each item from your in-basket and explain how each issue will be managed under the following headings:

a. Priority: Indicate what you consider your order of priority in dealing with each item.
b. Action: Indicate what will be done and approximately when.
c. Comments: Include any important details that may be relevant to your proposed action.

Give a brief indication of how you will plan your day using the time slots below.

9:00 a.m. _____

10:00 a.m. _____

11:00 a.m. _____

12 noon _____

1:00 p.m. _____

2:00 p.m. _____

3:00 p.m. _____

4:00 p.m. _____

5:00 p.m. _____

Work to take home _____

Figure 3.5   Workshop I: Fundraiser for a Fifth Grade Class Trip

---

Purpose:

- To raise money for the fifth grade trip to a local amusement park

Resources:

- Hard copy reference material including books on fundraising and a listing of local bus companies
- Access to computers for Internet research
- One complete afternoon without scheduled classes
- A parent advisor

Process:

The group works together to

- Set research tasks
- Decide on the format of the fundraiser
- Set the fundraising plan in motion
- Meet with the rest of the fifth grade to set the fund drive in motion

Debriefing:

- Process and product are evaluated by the group

Figure 3.6   Workshop II: An Eighth Grade Auto Shop Class

Purpose:

- To identify faults in a clutch mechanism of a standard shift car and to propose a course of corrective action

Resources:

- A faulty clutch mechanism
- Workshop manuals

Process:

- The group works together to identify faults and develop possible remedies.

Debriefing:

- The group's findings and solutions are discussed. The rest of the class evaluates the presentation using a presentation rubric.

Figure 3.7   Workshop III: A Senior Business Class

Purpose:

- To develop a SWOT (Strengths, Weaknesses, Opportunities, Threats) analysis for a firm

Resources:

- A description of the firm and the environment in which it operates
- Reference materials containing demographic, economic, and political information
- Materials to record ideas, conclusions, and so forth

Process:

- Teacher facilitates ground rules about time, behavior, and so forth.
- Group records the sum of its members' experiences and knowledge.
- Group gaps are identified.
- Tasks to fill gaps are agreed on and completed.
- SWOT analysis is completed and recorded for reporting back.

Debriefing:

- The SWOT analysis is discussed.
- Weaknesses and gaps are identified.
- The group process is evaluated.

Study Questions: Open or Closed

A *study question* is a device for focusing, guiding, and scoring an inquiry. Study questions may be closed, with one correct answer, or open, allowing for many possible answers. Study questions may also be narrow, allowing inquiry into one aspect of a topic or field over a short time, or broad, encouraging inquiry into a number of issues over a significant period of time. Study questions are useful when teachers want to have more control over their input to the problem-solving task, since these questions can be designed to have as few as a single correct outcome.

With study questions, it is the teacher/facilitator's job to

- Plan study questions that are motivating, are stimulating, and require an answer that is important to the topic
- Make sure the questions are answerable and the students possess the experience or skills with which to answer the questions
- Ascertain that students can answer the questions with the resources given in the time provided
- Make sure the question fits into a reasonable time frame
- Determine that the time and resources set aside are appropriate for the importance of the question in the overall topic of study
- Introduce the study question by first stating its purpose and then explaining how it fits into the overall study or topic

- Ensure that students know where and how to access resources
- Set or negotiate success criteria and methods for reporting back
- Facilitate the sharing of study questions through student reporting
- Evaluate the entire process with students

Figure 3.8 demonstrates how a study question can be used as a problem-based learning experience.

Figure 3.8   Study Question: How Many Square Feet to Live?

Directions:

Students will begin problem exploration by first discussing and exploring how much space various organisms need to survive. They can begin with how much room a cell needs to live. (In other words, students will explore the question of how big a human cell gets before it divides.) Students will advance their exploration by determining how much room different animals need to live.

Research:

Students will search different Web sites to determine habitat information for various animals (birds, fish, mammals, and so forth) to calculate how much room each needs to live in captivity. (An extension of this activity could involve addressing the question of how much room the animals use in the wild as opposed to in captivity.) This leads into the question of how much room the students themselves need to live.

Students will use spreadsheets to organize and analyze findings. In the spreadsheet, students will break down their definition of livable space. Then students will reevaluate their original estimation based on the reality of their findings.

The mathematical content of the project focuses on area and volume. Students will calculate area, surface area, and volume of different shapes as well as generate estimates on the amount of area volume needed to sustain life. Students will need to devise their own methods for measuring the surface area and volume for the shape of a cell. Students will also be asked to determine when the cell will divide.

Students will design and use an original model for taking any measurements needed to calculate the surface area and volume of their cell. They can also use computer programs to explore methods for determining surface areas. Once they have done this, teachers should ask students to present their findings to the class.

Evaluation:

The evaluation can be done using a rubric.

These five techniques—inquiry contracts, case studies, simulations, workshops, and study questions—demonstrate the various methods teachers can use to present a messy problem to students. Each of these techniques allows students to lead their own learning.

NEW ROLES FOR TEACHERS

The PBL techniques discussed on the previous pages show how the role of the classroom teacher is shifting from information giver to facilitator, guide, coach, and learner. As a facilitator, it is the teacher's role to provide a rich environment that involves students in high-level thought processes such as decision making and problem solving. This is best accomplished through collaborative group work, which encourages socialization and thus enhances learning (Dennick & Exley, 2004). The role of facilitator also requires that teachers provide varied activities to help students link new information to prior knowledge, provide opportunities for collaborative work, and engage students in inquiry and problem-solving activities through authentic learning tasks. Authentic tasks enable students to make necessary connections to real-world objects, events, and situations, since they mimic real-world problems. Teachers must also act as guides for their students, incorporating modeling as well as coaching into their repertoire. This type of guidance facilitates high-quality group interaction.

Modeling involves sharing one's thinking and demonstrating or explaining an idea, a concept, or a skill. In collaborative classrooms modeling enables teachers to share their thoughts regarding the content to be learned and to demonstrate to students how to communicate in collaborative learning situations. Modeling may involve thinking aloud (sharing thoughts about something) or demonstrating (showing students how to do something in a sequential manner).

Coaching involves giving hints or cues, providing feedback, redirecting student efforts, and helping students choose and employ various strategies. One of the most important functions of the teacher as coach is to scaffold student development. Effective caregivers regulate their dialogue with young children almost naturally. As these children learn, adults change the nature of their dialogue so that they continue to support the child while also giving the child increasing responsibility for the task. This type of teaching is called *scaffolding*. Scaffolding takes place within a child's zone of proximal development, a level or range in which a child can perform a task with help. Piaget (1954) refers to this concept as teachable moments: the adult is stretching the child's capacity but still keeps the information within the child's level of understanding. Scaffolding, then, is a technique wherein students are given just the right amount of help when they need it to enable them to retain as much responsibility for their own learning as possible.

In the inquiry-based collaborative classroom, the teacher shares authority with students in very specific ways. In most traditional classrooms, the teacher is largely, if not exclusively, responsible for setting goals, designing learning tasks, and assessing what is learned. In the inquiry-based collaborative classroom the teacher shares these responsibilities with students, becoming a colearner and coinvestigator right alongside them. The teacher invites students to set specific goals within the framework of what is being taught (such as researching specific information that is pertinent to the inquiry). The teacher provides options for activities and assignments that capture different student interests and goals and encourages students to assess what they learn through group reflection or self-reflection (Evensen & Hmelo, 2000). Collaborative facilitator-coaches encourage students to treat each other respectfully while focusing on high levels of understanding. They help students listen to diverse opinions, support knowledge claims with evidence, engage in critical and creative thinking, and participate in open and meaningful dialogue.

Collaborative classrooms tend to be noisier than traditional classrooms. Some teachers believe noisy classrooms indicate a lack of discipline or teacher control. In such situations, they argue, students cannot learn. However, truly collaborative classrooms do not lack structure; rather, they exemplify how good structure incorporates a manageable form of "organized chaos." In a collaborative classroom, students need opportunities to move about, talk, and ask questions—all in the name of research. The noise created in a smoothly running collaborative classroom is simply an indication that active learning is taking place.

Making a Shift in Teaching Practices

While teachers may need to act as facilitators and coaches to foster a successful PBL experience, Susan Florio-Ruane (1998) has observed that many teachers do not feel comfortable in these new roles. For many teachers, allowing students to initiate dialogue, determine topics, or explore perspectives other than their own may feel threatening at times. This reluctance to share control conflicts with the way effective caregivers teach their children in the home. Florio-Ruane and others have found that teachers often have difficulty helping students construct meaning, especially linking the new information to the prior knowledge and culture of the students. For many teachers this is in part because they believe their role is to transmit knowledge, and in part because they are held accountable for teaching discrete skills. When teachers are held accountable for teaching skills individually, they often do not teach them within a real-world context. The consequence is that these skills are less likely to become part of the learner's enduring knowledge base, thus impeding meaning making.

Until recently, much of schooling was built upon beliefs of teacher control and teacher-centered classrooms. This belief system assumes that properly managed instruction enables most students to acquire the skills and knowledge needed to continue to learn. Practice and repetition, with frequent tests of recall and recitation, characterize this approach. It is the only method many parents (and educators) have ever known, and the level of comfort many people have with this model makes it very difficult to supplant.

While curriculum reformers of the past would argue that process was always included in teaching practices, hands-on activities were generally eliminated in favor of more and more complex and abstract concepts. Many of today's educators entered the field during this period and still believe in focusing on content. Many educators argue that students' future success is contingent on their ability to read, write, and compute, and therefore these skills deserve the greatest emphasis. The curriculum and instruction strategies generated by this belief separate mathematics from science, often placing science outside of the "basics," except for certain facts and processes. In such a scheme, the time allocated for science instruction may not hold the same priority as reading, writing, and mathematics.

Recent neuroscientific and cognitive research aligns with the concept of learning as being an integrated activity. In addition, the standards documents of many professional organizations propose increasing emphasis on making connections within and among subject areas. When math and science are separated or, in certain cases, science is omitted entirely, the act of learning becomes more unnatural than natural. This results in teaching that works against the brain's natural ways of processing and learning new information. However, when instruction and learning are presented in an integrated manner and placed in a context that makes sense to the learner, the new learning has a much better chance of taking root at the deeper, conceptual level, being remembered, and being transferred to new and different situations. PBL is the kind of instruction that can help this happen (Torp & Sage, 2002).

Making a change from traditional methods of teaching requires leadership, support, and time. Staff development must address teachers' concerns about change, and teachers must first examine their assumptions about learning and then consider new curriculum guidelines. There is an intimate relationship among a teacher's definition of learning, his or her view of the content and scope of curricula, and his or her instructional practices. Examining assumptions honestly and forthrightly, in a supportive group, often helps to spur educators on toward the new paradigm.

Integrated Inquiry Project 1

MIDDLE/SECONDARY LEVELS: THE ROLLER COASTER

The following integrated inquiry project has been designed for advanced middle- and secondary-level students. It presents a project unit based on the real-world integration of math, science, and technology. The premise of this project is that a large national amusement park is sponsoring a competition with the goal of selecting a winning original model roller coaster. The model itself is to be made from everyday, basic materials (that is, toothpicks, craft sticks, metal tubing, and so on). The models submitted are required to be functional for demonstration purposes.

While this project explores the physics of roller coasters, it assumes some basic knowledge of physical science and provides a simplified view of the design and science considerations a mechanical design engineer takes into account in designing a roller coaster. It contains basic coaster dynamics such as constant acceleration and free-fall, forces, and motion in a circle, as well as the differentiation between speed, velocity, and acceleration. Aspects of this project require students to research some of these basic physics concepts. Many good Web sites devoted to the topic of "roller coaster physics" can be referenced by students as they create their designs. Students can also research roller coasters at school, university, and neighborhood libraries. (Additional research suggestions: contributions of Newton and Galileo to the physics of gravity, motion, and free-fall.)

To make this project "messier," teachers might suggest that students create a model for an innovative and original piece of playground equipment based on some of the physics concepts studied in this unit. Another idea might be to have students go to an actual amusement park and use some aspects of established ride designs to plan new playground equipment.

Project Standards (Grades 9–12)

 I. Mathematics Content Standards (Adapted From the National Council of Teachers of Mathematics, 2000)

Standard 1: Numbers and Operations

Instructional programs from pre-kindergarten through grade 12 should enable all students to

- Understand numbers, ways of representing numbers, relationships among numbers, and number systems
- Understand the meaning of operations and how they relate to one another
- Compute fluently and make reasonable estimates

Standard 2: Algebra

Instructional programs from pre-kindergarten through grade 12 should enable all students to

- Understand patterns, relations, and functions
- Represent and analyze mathematical situations and structures using algebraic symbols
- Use mathematical models to represent and understand quantitative relationships
- Analyze change in various contexts

Standard 3: Geometry

Instructional programs from pre-kindergarten through grade 12 should enable all students to

- Analyze characteristics and properties of two- and three-dimensional geometric shapes and develop arguments about relationships
- Use visualization, spatial reasoning, and geometric modeling to solve problems

Standard 4: Measurement

Instructional programs from pre-kindergarten through grade 12 should enable all students to

- Understand attributes, units, and systems of measurement
- Apply a variety of techniques, tools, and formulas for determining measurements

Standard 6: Problem Solving

Instructional programs from pre-kindergarten through grade 12 should enable all students to

- Build new mathematical knowledge through problem solving
- Solve problems that arise in mathematics and in other contexts
- Apply and adapt a wide variety of strategies to solve problems
- Monitor and reflect on the process of mathematical problem solving

Standard 7: Reasoning and Proof

Instructional programs from pre-kindergarten through grade 12 should enable all students to

- Make and investigate mathematical conjectures
- Select and use various types of reasoning and methods of proof

Standard 8: Communication

Instructional programs from pre-kindergarten through grade 12 should enable all students to

- Organize and consolidate their mathematical thinking through communication
- Communicate their mathematical thinking coherently and clearly to peers, teachers, and others
- Analyze and evaluate the mathematical thinking and strategies of others
- Use the language of mathematics to express mathematical ideas precisely

Standard 9: Connections

Instructional programs from pre-kindergarten through grade 12 should enable all students to

- Recognize and use connections among mathematical ideas
- Recognize and apply mathematics in contexts outside of mathematics

Standard 10: Representation

Instructional programs from pre-kindergarten through grade 12 should enable all students to

- Create and use representations to organize, record, and communicate mathematical ideas
- Select, apply, and translate among mathematical representations to solve problems
- Use representations to model and interpret physical, social, and mathematical phenomena

II. Science Content Standards (Adapted From the *National Science Education Standards*, 1995)

Content Standard A: Science as Inquiry

Students should develop:

- Abilities necessary to do scientific inquiry
- Understandings about scientific inquiry

Content Standard B: Physical Science

Students should develop an understanding of:

- Motions and forces
- Interactions of energy and matter

Content Standard E: Science and Technology

Students should develop:

- Abilities of technological design
- Understandings about science and technology

Content Standard F: Science in Personal and Social Perspectives

Students should develop an understanding of:

- Science and technology in local, national, and global challenges

Content Standard G: History and Nature of Science

Students should develop an understanding of:

- Science as a human endeavor
- Nature of scientific knowledge
- Historical perspectives

III. Technology Foundation Standards (International Society for Technology in Education [ISTE]) (Adapted From the *National Educational Technology Standards [NETS] Project*, 1998)

Basic Operations and Concepts

- Students demonstrate a sound understanding of the nature and operation of technology systems.
- Students are proficient in the use of technology.

Technology Productivity Tools

- Students use technology tools to enhance learning, increase productivity, and promote creativity.
- Students use productivity tools to collaborate in constructing technology-enhanced models, preparing publications, and producing other creative works.

Technology Communications Tools

- Students use telecommunications to collaborate, publish, and interact with peers, experts, and other audiences.
- Students use a variety of media and formats to communicate information and ideas effectively to multiple audiences.

Technology Research Tools

- Students use technology to locate, evaluate, and collect information from a variety of sources.
- Students evaluate and select new information resources and technological innovations based on the appropriateness to specific tasks.

Technology Problem-Solving and Decision-Making Tools

- Students use technology resources for solving problems and making informed decisions.
- Students employ technology in the development of strategies for solving problems in the real world.

Performance Task

Teachers should tell students that a large national amusement park is sponsoring a contest to see who can best design and construct a model roller coaster made from everyday, basic materials (that is, toothpicks, craft sticks, metal tubing, and so on). The coaster should give the sensation of speed, acceleration, and danger while maintaining a safe ride. Teachers should explain that students must develop functional completed models so that they can demonstrate their various coaster designs.

Teachers may want to supply the information in Figure 3.9 to students so that they can familiarize themselves with background information about roller coasters prior to the first class.

Figure 3.9   Background Information: How Does a Roller Coaster Work?

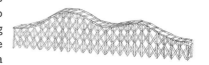

What many people do not realize as they're whizzing down the tracks of a roller coaster at 60 miles an hour is that a roller coaster has no engine. The coaster is pulled to the top of the first hill at the beginning of the ride, but after that it must complete the ride on its own. The coaster isn't propelled around the track by a motor or pulled by a hitch. The conversion of potential energy to kinetic energy is what drives the roller coaster, and all of the kinetic energy needed for the ride is present once the coaster descends the first hill.

An electric motor pulls the coaster to the top of the first hill. After the coaster has been pulled to the top, no more external energy is added to it. The amount of energy the coaster has to complete its journey around the track depends on the potential energy it has due to its height at the top of its first hill and the beginning of its descent. There is a relationship between the height of this hill and the speed of the coaster. The shape of the first hill determines how fast the coaster can safely travel on the track and also determines whether or not the coaster will stay on the track.

Once the coaster has gained momentum, different types of wheels help keep the ride smooth. Running wheels guide the coaster on the track. Friction wheels control lateral motion (movement to either side of the track). A final set of wheels keeps the coaster on the track even if it's inverted.

Project Instructions

This project can be started by first having students read to themselves the project introduction information describing the workings of a roller coaster (see Figure 3.10). This project is meant to be a culminating project that follows basic physical science instruction on information such as the difference between velocity and acceleration. In addition, students need to learn a simplified version of both the design and science considerations that a mechanical design engineer takes into account when designing an amusement park roller coaster. (This aspect of the project might be best developed by inviting a guest speaker to the class who has had some mechanical design engineering experience.)

Students should read the project introduction to themselves, discuss the information within their small groups, and then share the small-group discourse during a full class discussion.

Teachers should also read and/or give the information in Figure 3.11 to students.

Figure 3.10   Introduction: The Physical Science of Roller Coasters

The roller coaster is a balance between safety and sensation. The ride must be as safe as possible while still providing a sensation of danger. Safety is of the utmost concern, since any reported injuries result in fewer riders and a short life span for that particular roller coaster. The key to a successful coaster is to give the rider the sensation of speed, acceleration, and danger while keeping the ride safe. What this means is that designing a successful roller coaster is simply a matter of speed control. To achieve this control, the hills, curves, dips, straight-aways, braking systems, and loops are not randomly designed. They follow some simple rules of physics.

To understand how all this fits together, teams must first learn some basic physical science such as the difference between velocity and acceleration. In addition, teams need a simplified version of both the design and science considerations a mechanical design engineer takes into account when designing an amusement park roller coaster.

Velocity

Velocity describes how quickly an object can change its position. The higher the velocity, the quicker the object travels between two locations. Phrases such as "how fast" or "how quickly" are used to describe velocity. In everyday speech the word *speed* is commonly substituted for velocity. However, technically the two are different. In actuality, velocity is speed along with direction. For example, when east is the direction and 55 mph is the speed, velocity is shown in the following formula:

$$\text{Velocity} = \frac{\text{Units of Distance}}{\text{Units of Time}}$$

Acceleration

Acceleration describes the rate at which an object can change its velocity. Phrases such as *speed up, change speed,* and *change velocity* are used to describe acceleration. If students are in doubt as to whether or not they are visualizing acceleration or a constant velocity along a straight line, all they have to do is ask themselves one question: "Is the object slowing down or speeding up?" If the answer is "Speeding up," then the object is accelerating. If the answer is "Slowing down," then the object is moving with a constant velocity. Acceleration is shown in the following formula:

$$\text{Acceleration} = \frac{\text{Units of Distance}}{(\text{Units of Time})^2} = \frac{\text{Units of Velocity}}{\text{Units of Time}}$$

Figure 3.11   Background Information: How Does a Roller Coaster Work?

The basic roller coaster started with Galileo Galilei. Galileo's experiment can be demonstrated by constructing a roller coaster model using a HotWheels® track and a marble. This model demonstrates that the marble can take any path until it reaches the same height it started from, assuming there is no friction. (If the marble does not roll to the same height it started from, it is because of friction; otherwise, it consistently rolls to the same height.)

The marble begins to roll down due to the force of gravity and stops when all the gravitational energy is used up. The marble accelerates only while a force acts on it in its direction of motion. The acceleration can be demonstrated experimentally using the HotWheels track. If a long enough section is made horizontal, it can be shown that the average velocities calculated at the beginning and at the end of the horizontal section are equal. The marble will accelerate along the drop and move at a constant velocity along the horizontal section and slow down as it climbs up the opposite side. When the marble slows down and speeds up on the hills it is visually obvious. What is not so visually obvious is what happens along the horizontal section of the track. The marble's constant velocity can be shown mathematically. If the horizontal section of the track is divided into two sections, the average velocity of the marble along these two sections can be calculated. If this is done accurately, the velocities will be nearly equal. Fairly long sections of horizontal track can be used to obtain more accurate results, since the longer the sections of track, the greater the time measurements and the lower the percentage of errors.

Along the horizontal section of the track—ignoring the minimal effects of friction—there are no forces horizontally acting on the marble. Therefore, the marble moves at a constant velocity while no force acts upon it.

A roller coaster is called a *coaster* because once it gets started, it coasts over the entire track. No outside forces are required for most coasters. Roller coasters trade height for velocity and velocity for height. Most calculations rely on using velocity measurements in one way or another. The first step is to calculate the changes in speed. In an ideal world, mechanical energy is conserved. Mechanical energy on a roller coaster comes in two basic forms: Kinetic energy, $KE = (1/2)mv^2$ (1/2 momentum × velocity), and potential energy, $PE = mgh$ (momentum × gravity × height), due to gravity. Total energy, ET, is conserved and is equal to the sum of kinetic and potential energy at any single location. $ET = KE + PE$ (at any single location).

To calculate a change in velocity associated with a change in height, you must first identify two locations of interest: one location with both a speed and a height and the other with either speed or height. Next, you would write an equation setting the total energy at one location equal to the total energy at the other location. Finally, you would solve for the unknown variable.

Example: First hill = height 90m

Second hill = height 70m

Velocity (*v*) = 9.4m/s

Gravity (*g*) = 9.8

1. What is the velocity at the bottom of the first hill?

$$ET(top) = ET(bottom)$$
$$KE + PE = KE + PE$$
$$(1/2)mv^2 + mgh = (1/2)mv^2 + mgh$$
$$(1/2)v^2 + gh = (1/2)mv^2 + mgh$$

(Continued)

Figure 3.11 (Continued)

The masses cancel out because the coaster is the same at the top and bottom.

$$(1/2)v^2 + gh = (1/2)v^2 + gh$$

Substitute the numbers at each location.

$$(1/2)(9.4)^2 + 9.8(90) = (1/2)v^2 + 9.8(0)$$

The height at the bottom is zero because it is the lowest point when compared to the starting height.

$$4.18 + 882 = (1/2)v^2$$
$$926.18 = (1/2)v^2$$
$$1852.36 = v^2$$

v = 43.04 m/s at the bottom of the first hill. What is the velocity at the top of the second hill?

$$ET(\text{top of 1st hill}) = ET(\text{top of 2nd hill})$$
$$KE + PE = KE + PE$$
$$(1/2)mv^2 + mgh = (1/2)mv^2 + mgh$$
$$(1/2)v^2 + gh = (1/2)mv^2 + mgh$$

The masses cancel out because it is the same coaster at the top and bottom.

$$(1/2)v^2 + gh = (1/2)v^2 + gh$$

Substitute the numbers at each location.

$$(1/2)(9.4)^2 + 9.8(90) = (1/2)v^2 + 9.8(70)$$

Notice all the numbers on the left side come from the top of the first hill, while all the numbers on the right side come from the top of the second hill.

$$44.18 + 882 = (1/2)v^2 + 686$$
$$926.18 = (1/2)v^2$$
$$240.18 = (1/2)v^2$$
$$120.09 = v^2$$
$$v = 10.96 \text{ m/s at the top of the second hill}$$

This technique can be used to calculate the velocity anywhere along the coaster.

Getting the Coaster Started

Some outside force has to act upon the coaster to get it started. In the first example, some energy power has been added to get the coaster up to 9.4 m/s. This is accomplished by doing work on the coaster. A simplified definition of work would be force times displacement when the force and displacement go in the same direction. When the force acting on the coaster and the displacement of the coaster are in the same direction, work adds energy to the coaster. When the force acting on the coaster and the displacement of the coaster are in opposite directions, work removes energy from the coaster (as in braking).

$$\text{Work} = (\text{Force})(\text{Displacement})$$
$$W = Fd$$

Teachers can ask students the following questions to get the discussion started:

- What kinds of outside forces are used to get various coasters started?
- How would you incorporate this information into your coaster design?

Teachers should provide the information in Figure 3.12 to students for use as reference material during the design phase of the unit. All these forces need to be considered by students when they are designing their coasters.

Figure 3.12 Considerations When Designing a Roller Coaster

Projectile Motion and Roller Coaster Hills

A free-fall hill shape gives a roller coaster rider a weightless sensation. To achieve this weightless sensation, the hill is designed to have the same shape as the path of a ball being thrown off the top of a hill. Shape is determined by how fast the roller coaster car travels over the hill. The faster the coaster travels over the hill, the wider the hill must be. Incorporate this concept into your coaster design.

The Thrill of Free-Fall

There comes a certain point on the free-fall drop where the track must redirect the riders, otherwise the riders will just plummet to the ground. This point is the transition point from free-fall to controlled acceleration. This point is also the maximum angle of a hill. This angle can be in virtually any range from 35° to 55°.

For the bottom section of the track, the new equation has the desired outcome of changing the direction of the coaster from a downward motion to a purely horizontal motion. The track must apply a vertical component of velocity to reduce the coaster's vertical velocity to zero. The track also must increase the horizontal velocity of the coaster to the value determined from energy relationships.

Loops and Double Loops

The average person has usually heard of centrifugal force. When asked to describe what it is, people often say it is the force that pushes an object to the outside of a curve or circle. However, this definition is incorrect. Actually, there is no force at work pushing an object to the outside. The terms *centrifugal* and *centripetal* refer to opposite forces. While centrifugal force refers to outward movement (movement away from center), centripetal force refers to inward direction or movement toward center.

When a person is riding in a car that makes a sharp turn, that person perceives some force as pushing him or her to the outside of the curve. But what force is physically pushing the person? If frictional forces oppose the direction of motion, can it be friction? Keep the following questions in mind when creating your projects:

- What is centripetal force?
- How is it the same as centrifugal force?
- How is it different?
- How would you incorporate either or both of these forces into your roller coaster loop design?

Note: Motion along a curve or through a circle is always caused by a centripetal force. This is a force that pushes an object in an inward direction. The moon orbits the Earth in a circular motion because the force of gravity pulls on the moon in an inward direction toward the center of its orbit. In a roller coaster loop, riders are pushed inward toward the center of the loop by forces resulting from the car seat (at the loop's bottom) and by gravity (at the loop's top).

Figure 3.13   Project Vocabulary

Acceleration

Objects that are changing their speed or their direction are accelerating. The rate at which the speed or direction changes is referred to as acceleration.

Balanced and unbalanced forces

A balanced force results whenever two or more forces act upon an object in such a way as to exactly counteract each other. As a person sits in his or her seat, the seat pushes upward with a force equal in strength and opposite in direction to the force of gravity. These two forces are said to balance each other, causing the person to remain at rest. If the seat is suddenly pulled out from under the person, he or she experiences an unbalanced force. There is no longer an upward seat force to balance the downward pull of gravity, so the person accelerates to the ground.

Energy

Energy comes in many forms. The two most important forms for coasters are kinetic energy and potential energy. In the absence of external forces such as air resistance and friction, the total amount of an object's energy remains constant. On a coaster ride, energy is rapidly transformed from potential energy to kinetic energy when falling, and from kinetic energy to potential energy when rising. However, the total amount of energy remains constant during both rising and falling.

Force

A force is a push or a pull acting upon an object. Forces result from interactions between two objects. Some forces can act from a distance without actual contact between the two interacting objects. Gravity is one such force. On a free-fall ride, a force of gravitational attraction exists between Earth and an individual's body even though Earth and that individual's body are not in contact.

Friction

Friction is a force that resists the motion of an object. Friction results from the close interaction between two surfaces that are sliding across each other. When a person slams on the brakes and the car skids to a stop with locked wheels, it is the force of friction that brings the car to a stop. Friction resists the car's motion.

"g"

The letter "g" is a unit of acceleration equal to the acceleration caused by gravity. Gravity causes free-falling objects on Earth to change their speeds at rates of about 10 m/s each second (equivalent to a change in speed of 32 ft/s in each consecutive second). If an object is said to experience 3 g's of acceleration, then the object is changing its speed at a rate of about 30 m/s every second.

Inertia

Inertia is the tendency of an object to resist change in its state of motion. More massive objects have more inertia, which means they have a stronger tendency to resist changes in the way they are moving and require more force to change their state of motion.

Kinetic energy

Kinetic energy is the energy possessed by an object because of its motion. All moving objects have kinetic energy. The amount of kinetic energy depends upon the mass and speed of the object. A roller coaster car has a lot of kinetic energy if it is moving fast and has a lot of mass. In general, the kinetic energy of a roller coaster rider is at a maximum when the rider reaches a minimum height.

Mass

The mass of an object is a measurement of the amount of material in a substance. Mass refers to the amount of substance an object may possess.

Momentum

Momentum is the quantity of motion an object possesses. Any mass that is in motion has momentum. In fact, momentum depends upon mass and velocity, or, in other words, the amount of substance that is moving and the speed with which that substance is moving. For example, a train of roller coaster cars moving at a high speed has a lot of momentum, while a building, despite its large mass, has no momentum since it is at rest.

Speed

Speed is a measurement of how fast an object is moving. Fast-moving objects can cover large distances in a small amount of time.

Velocity

The velocity of an object refers to the speed and direction in which it moves. If a person drives north to his or her workplace and the speedometer reads 35 miles per hour, then his or her velocity is 35 miles per hour in a northward direction. Velocity is speed with a direction.

Weight

Weight is a measurement of the gravitational force acting on an object. The weight of an object is expressed in pounds in the United States. A 180-pound person experiences a force of gravitational attraction to Earth equal to 180 pounds.

Weightlessness

Weightlessness is the sensation people experience when they no longer feel external forces acting upon their bodies. For example, at the top of the first hill on a roller coaster, a 120-pound rider feels 120 pounds of force from the seat acting as an external force upon his or her body. (Each rider feels his or her normal weight.) However, as the car begins its descent from the hill's summit, the seat falls out from under the rider and he or she no longer feels the external force of the seat, and thus he or she experiences a brief sensation of weightlessness. The rider has not lost any weight, but feels as though he or she has because of the absence of the seat force. In this context, weightlessness is a sensation and not an actual change in weight.

Teachers can use the vocabulary in Figure 3.13 in one of two ways. It can be used for background class discussion or teachers can simply give students a list of these terms for use as reference material.

Presentation

All models can be set up for demonstration simultaneously, and designers can explain the finer points to the audience according to a predetermined schedule. While the teacher does the overall project evaluation, students also have input into each other's evaluations using a common rubric (see Figure 3.14). (See Chapter 5 for more information on rubrics.)

Figure 3.14 Roller Coaster Rubric

Name: _____ Section: _____ Date: _____

Excellent (E)

_____ The coaster design is creative, functional, and viable.

_____ The mathematics are complete, accurate, and carried beyond the basic project requirements.

_____ Each partner is well prepared and contributes to the design presentation.

_____ The presentation has a clear beginning, middle, and end.

Satisfactory (S)

_____ The coaster is functional and viable (the coaster works) but is not especially creative or unique.

_____ Most of the mathematics are accurate.

_____ Both members contribute something of value.

_____ The presentation makes sense and holds my attention.

Unsatisfactory (U)

_____ The coaster design has been poorly envisioned and as a result, the coaster won't function as it should.

_____ The mathematics are incomplete and/or inaccurate.

_____ Both partners do not contribute equally.

Explain the reason for the grade you gave in four or five complete sentences.

_____

_____

_____

_____

Resources

The following Web sites can be used by both teachers and students to gather ideas and information regarding roller coasters. All the sites offer information on roller coaster design, discussion forums, photos, news sources, and links to related Web sites.

www.rollercoaster.com

www.joyrides.com

www.ultimaterollercoaster.com

www.aceonline.org/links

science.howstuffworks.com/roller-coaster.htm

www.coaster.net

www.britannica.com/coasters/ride.html

www.fearofphysics.com/Roller/roller.html

INTEGRATED INQUIRY PROJECT 2

SECONDARY LEVEL: BUILDING BRIDGES

The following integrated inquiry project has been designed for middle- to secondary-level students. It presents a project unit based on the real-world integration of math, science, and technology. The premise of this project unit is that student teams are to have the experience of designing and constructing their own bridge using principles learned from physics, functions, and calculus. Project directions lead students from the initial step of brainstorming ideas for potential designs through the presentation of the completed model.

Project Standards (Grades 9–12)

I. Mathematics Content Standards (Adapted From the National Council of Teachers of Mathematics, 2000)

Standard 1: Numbers and Operations

Instructional programs from pre-kindergarten through grade 12 should enable all students to

- Understand numbers, ways of representing numbers, relationships among numbers, and number systems
- Understand the meaning of operations and how they relate to one another
- Compute fluently and make reasonable estimates

Standard 2: Patterns, Functions, and Algebra

Instructional programs from pre-kindergarten through grade 12 should enable all students to

- Understand patterns, relations, and functions
- Represent and analyze mathematical situations and structures using algebraic symbols
- Use mathematical models to represent and understand quantitative relationships
- Analyze change in various contexts

Standard 3: Geometry

Instructional programs from pre-kindergarten through grade 12 should enable all students to

- Analyze characteristics and properties of two- and three-dimensional geometric shapes and develop arguments about relationships
- Use visualization, spatial reasoning, and geometric modeling

Standard 4: Measurement

Instructional programs from pre-kindergarten through grade 12 should enable all students to

- Understand attributes, units, and systems of measurement
- Apply a variety of techniques, tools, and formulas for determining measurements

Standard 5: Data Analysis and Probability

Instructional programs from pre-kindergarten through grade 12 should enable all students to

- Develop and evaluate inferences and predictions that are based on data

Standard 6: Problem Solving

Instructional programs from pre-kindergarten through grade 12 should enable all students to

- Build new mathematical knowledge through problem solving
- Solve problems that arise in mathematics and in other contexts
- Apply and adapt a wide variety of strategies to solve problems
- Monitor and reflect on the process of mathematical problem solving

Standard 7: Reasoning and Proof

Instructional programs from pre-kindergarten through grade 12 should enable all students to

- Make and investigate mathematical conjectures
- Select and use various types of reasoning and methods of proof

Standard 8: Communication

Instructional programs from pre-kindergarten through grade 12 should enable all students to

- Organize and consolidate their mathematical thinking through communication
- Communicate their mathematical thinking coherently and clearly to peers, teachers, and others
- Analyze and evaluate the mathematical thinking and strategies of others
- Use the language of mathematics to express mathematical ideas precisely

Standard 9: Connections

Instructional programs from pre-kindergarten through grade 12 should enable all students to

- Recognize and use connections among mathematical ideas
- Understand how mathematical ideas interconnect and build on one another to produce a coherent whole
- Recognize and apply mathematics in contexts outside of mathematics

Standard 10: Representation

Instructional programs from pre-kindergarten through grade 12 should enable all students to

- Create and use representations to organize, record, and communicate mathematical ideas
- Use representations to model and interpret physical, social, and mathematical phenomena

II. Science Content Standards (Adapted From the *National Science Education Standards*, 1995)

Content Standard A: Science as Inquiry

Students should develop:

- Abilities necessary to do scientific inquiry
- Understandings about scientific inquiry

Content Standard B: Physical Science

Students should develop an understanding of:

- Motions and forces
- Interactions of energy and matter

Content Standard D: Earth and Space

Students should develop an understanding of:

- Energy in the Earth system

Content Standard E: Science and Technology

Students should develop:

- Abilities of technological design
- Understandings about science and technology

Content Standard F: Science in Personal and Social Perspectives

Students should develop an understanding of:

- Science and technology in local, national, and global challenges

Content Standard G: History and Nature of Science

Students should develop an understanding of:

- Science as a human endeavor
- Nature of scientific knowledge
- Historical perspectives

III. Technology Foundation Standards (International Society for Technology in Education [ISTE]) (Adapted From the *National Educational Technology Standards [NETS] Project*, 1998)

Basic Operations and Concepts

- Students demonstrate a sound understanding of the nature and operation of technology systems.
- Students are proficient in the use of technology.

Technology Productivity Tools

- Students use technology tools to enhance learning, increase productivity, and promote creativity.
- Students use productivity tools to collaborate in constructing technology-enhanced models, preparing publications, and producing other creative works.

Technology Communications Tools

- Students use telecommunications to collaborate, publish, and interact with peers, experts, and other audiences.
- Students use a variety of media and formats to communicate information and ideas effectively to multiple audiences.

Technology Research Tools

- Students use technology to locate, evaluate, and collect information from a variety of sources.

- Students use technology tools to process data and report results.
- Students evaluate and select new information resources and technological innovations based on the appropriateness to specific tasks.

Technology Problem-Solving and Decision-Making Tools

- Students use technology resources for solving problems and making informed decisions.
- Students employ technology in the development of strategies for solving problems in the real world.

Performance Task

Students are to work in teams of two to design and construct a bridge according to the design parameters. Once the assorted team models have been completed, students are to measure the mass of their bridge construction and then test the load capacity. The teacher may provide a spring scale and weights to facilitate the process, but it is up to the students to determine just how the testing is to be carried out. Teams are then to analyze the available data and determine the relationship between the mass and load capacity of the bridges. This information is to be made available to the entire class so that the class can decide which team bridge design is best. (Students should be prepared to justify their design choices.) Completed models can be presented at a bridge expo.

The background information (see Figure 3.15) is to be handed out to student teams so that they can begin to brainstorm ideas prior to a class discussion of the assignment parameters.

Figure 3.15   Background Information: Constructing Bridges

The State Highway Commission is sponsoring a bridge-building contest to help students become more involved in their communities as well as increase their awareness of transportation needs. The objective of this contest is to design and build a bridge that can support a maximum load while using a minimum of resources. The contest design parameters are as follows:

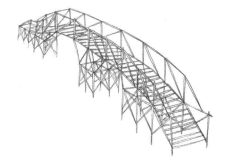

- The construction is to consist of only toothpicks and glue.
- The bridge must cover a minimum span of 30 centimeters.
- You may use cement glue to fix the toothpicks together (this should be done only at the joint areas; entire toothpicks should not be covered with glue).
- You may use up to 1,000 toothpicks in your design.
- The toothpicks may be shortened, bent, blunted, or spliced.

Presentation

All models can be set up for demonstration simultaneously and designers can explain the finer points to the audience according to a predetermined schedule. In this project as with the others, the teacher is the guide on the side, acting only as the facilitator. While the teacher does the overall project evaluation, students also have input into each other's evaluations through a common rubric (teachers could use a rubric similar to the one used in the roller coaster project).

The background research questions in Figure 3.16 have been designed to help students focus their research. By asking themselves these questions, student teams have an idea as to where to begin the background inquiry. Teachers can give these questions to students or read the questions aloud.

Vocabulary

Teachers can use the definitions listed in Figure 3.17 for class discussion or they can supply the terms to the students as reference material.

Resources

Students can use the following Web sites, which all contain activities and resources for the study of bridges, as a starting point for research forays and as a way to find links to related sites.

www.exploratorium.edu/science_explorer/index.html

www.eweek.org

www.pbs.org/wgbh/nova/bridge/resources.html

www.discoverengineering.org/home.asp

Project Extension

The following project extension can be used with students who are not sufficiently challenged by the class assignment or students who complete the assignment well in advance of the rest of the class.

Some engineering principles used in bridge building are also used in the design and construction of other structures. For an extension project, teachers can ask students to study the engineering principles behind the three primary types of bridges and then research how these same principles are also used in the design and construction of other structures. Each of the teams can then create models of their researched structures. A description of the structure and its use should accompany each model exhibited.

Figure 3.16   Background Research Focus Questions

1. What are some of the primary factors engineers must consider as they design a bridge?

2. The collapse of the Tacoma Narrows Bridge was a catastrophic yet educational event. What were the unique environmental factors engineers overlooked when they designed this bridge?

3. Describe how bridges have affected communities both economically and socially.

4. Discuss the three primary families of bridges. Describe how their structures distribute the load the bridge must support.

5. Define *force* and *equilibrium*. Describe the forces that act on a bridge. Discuss why it is important for the forces acting on a bridge to be in a state of equilibrium.

6. Discuss why suspension bridges have enabled engineers to design and construct bridges that span great lengths and why arch and beam bridges are not feasible technologies for long-spanning bridges.

7. Earthquakes are only one kind of natural disaster that can cause a great deal of damage to bridges. What kinds of modifications can engineers make to their bridge to minimize this kind of damage? (Any idea is acceptable as long as it can be supported with a logical rationale.)

8. Some engineers feel too much effort, time, and money go into the design and construction of bridges that have unique and often breathtaking appearances. Discuss why appearance is important to communities and why design engineers may have a different perspective.

Figure 3.17   Project Vocabulary

Anchorage

That which makes something secure; a mooring.

Composite

A complex material, such as wood or fiberglass, in which two or more distinct, structurally complementary substances, especially metals, ceramics, glasses, and polymers, combine to produce structural or functional properties not present in any individual component.

Compression

The act or state of pressing together.

Load

The overall force to which a structure is subjected in supporting a weight or mass or in resisting externally applied forces.

Oscillate

To swing back and forth with a steady, uninterrupted rhythm.

Propagate

To spread to a larger area or greater number; to disseminate.

Resonate

To reinforce oscillations because the natural frequency of the device is the same as the frequency of the source.

Tension

The act or process of stretching something tight.

Viaduct

A series of spans or arches used to carry a road or railroad over a wide valley or over other roads or railroads.

Planning Problem-Based Learning for the Classroom

In previous chapters, the educational significance of problem-based learning (PBL) was explained in depth, along with the structure used for implementing such a program. In this chapter, teachers are guided through the process of carrying out a PBL experience and are presented with ideas for incorporating PBL into their existing curricula.

PLANNING FOR INTEGRATED LEARNING

The best way for teachers to begin creating a PBL experience is to use a planning outline (see Figure 4.1) that covers all the important aspects of a PBL experience. To better understand planning strategies, teachers may want to begin by applying the questions posed in the outline to a past unit, since the topic will already be familiar. The outline in Figure 4.1 should serve only as a general guide; not every question is applicable to every project.

The following example demonstrates how one teacher used the guidelines given in the outline in Figure 4.1 to prepare a PBL project that met her curriculum needs.

The teacher in this example, Ms. Jones, is a sixth grade math teacher who is working on a graphing unit with her class and wants to increase her students' understanding of how different graphs can be developed and employed. She decides her topic will be surveys, and she begins creating her problem by

Figure 4.1   Planning Outline

I.   Concepts

When contemplating concepts, consider the following:

- On which important math and science concepts should this unit focus?
- In what ways are these concepts defined?
- What might be referred to as "the big ideas"?

II.   Processes

Decide which of the following processes to include (one process or several can be included, depending on the unit):

- Thinking
- Collecting data
- Analyzing data
- Drawing conclusions
- Representing knowledge

III.   Generalizations

Use the following questions to identify ways in which these concepts can be connected or combined to form the kinds of generalizations mathematicians and scientists accept as true and important.

- Which relationships among these concepts are relevant?
- What are the characteristics, definitions, examples, and/or categories that distinguish each of the concepts?
- What are similarities and/or differences among the concepts?
- What are some of the consequences, causes, effects, and/or predictions that can be made based upon these concepts or processes?
- Under what conditions or in which contexts will these concepts exist or be accomplished?
- Upon what assumptions are these concepts based?

IV.   Theory

Design a way these assumptions can be linked so as to form a theory that is true and important to know.

V.   Performance Tasks or Products

Decide on the kinds of performance tasks or products students will create to demonstrate their learning (their mastery of the science and math content and processes used). Ask:

- Will students be using the skills and knowledge scientists, engineers, designers, and other professionals use in the creation of this performance task or product?
- How does this task or product relate to the developmental needs and interests of the students?
- What are the specific qualities and characteristics that must be contained in the evidence of learning?
- How will production, perception, and reflection be documented?

VI.   Assessment

Decide how the evidence of learning will be assessed. Ask:

- What kind of authentic and alternative assessment measures will be used?
- What criteria (rubric and benchmarks) will be used for assessing students' products?
- Will the products be the kind that fit the portfolio profile? (Do they conform to the requirements and/or parameters of a portfolio?)

VII.   Lesson Plans

Map out a series of lesson plans for the unit design. Ask:

- What will students do to learn?
- What resources will be used?
- How are these lessons related to students' interests?
- How are these lessons related to students' needs?
- What questions will they ask?

VIII.   Questioning Strategies

Decide on the questioning strategies to be employed. Ask:

- What questions should be asked to help students define concepts?
- What questions should be asked to help students link concepts to meaningful generalizations?
- What questions should be asked to help students identify evidence that the generalizations are true?

determining that the concepts and big ideas important to this topic are measurement gathering, collating, and analyzing the data and representing that data. The processes Ms. Jones wishes to include are collecting data, analyzing data, and drawing conclusions. By asking herself, "Which relationships among these concepts are relevant?" and determining that they all involve uses of data, Ms. Jones is able to identify ways in which these concepts can be connected. Ms. Jones decides the performance task will be for students to create graphs that represent the survey data. She wants the graphs to be accurate representations of the data gathered by the students as well as representative of the conclusions drawn from the data. Ms. Jones's task relates to student interest because sixth graders are very interested in learning about the opinions of their peers, which they will discover from the results of the surveys. The specific qualities and characteristics Ms. Jones decides the students should include in their evidence of learning for this unit are accurate data records and accurately constructed graphs that illustrate the conclusions of the surveys. Ms. Jones decides to use student activity logs to document students' production, perceptions, and reflection. She also decides to use group and individual reflections for this purpose.

Ms. Jones decides to assess the evidence of learning with a rubric measuring the following characteristics:

- Knowledge of data-recording methods
- Accuracy in data recording
- Accuracy of graph construction and selection
- Clarity of the graph
- Graph creativity and originality
- Teamwork and cooperation

An example of the rubric Ms. Jones developed to assess this project is shown in Figure 4.2.

GUIDELINES FOR IMPLEMENTING A PROBLEM-BASED LEARNING PROJECT

The characteristics, approaches, and aspects of PBL that have been discussed in this and previous chapters can be combined into guidelines teachers can use as a framework for designing and implementing their own PBL projects. The following steps provide a helpful guide teachers can follow when setting up a PBL project.

Step 1. The teacher begins the PBL process by developing a real-world, open-ended, and messy problem: a problem without a clear-cut solution. This problem should relate to the unit that is being taught in that it should involve the application of the content skills and concepts covered.

Step 2. After the teacher has chosen a messy and authentic problem, he or she needs to think of ways in which students can use different research methods and tools in their quest for a solution to the problem. Some research options might include conducting research through the Internet, contacting

Figure 4.2   Rubric for Survey Graph

Criteria	Novice	Basic	Proficient	Advanced
Data-recording methods	Methods indicate little understanding of data recording	Methods demonstrate partial understanding of data recording	Methods demonstrate competence in all aspects of data recording	Methods demonstrate a high level of competence and sophistication in all aspects of data recording
Data-recording accuracy	Data recorded with little or no accuracy	Data recorded with some degree of accuracy	Data recorded with a high level of accuracy	All data recorded with total and complete accuracy
Graph construction and selection	Wrong choice of graph, poor construction	Correct graph selected, but construction is flawed	Correct graph choice and construction	Extremely well-constructed graph with no errors or detractions of any kind
Graph clarity	Totally confusing and misleading	Some parts of graph make sense but others are confusing	Easy to read and understand	Extremely high level of clarity allows for sophisticated inferences and extensions
Graph creativity	Poor use of color Absence of detail	Some color used Some detail included	Neat presentation makes good use of color and detail	Original presentation uses clean lines, vibrant color, and high level of detail
Teamwork and cooperation	Little or no cooperation evident	Team worked together intermittently	Team worked well together	Team members developed a synergistic dynamic

possible sources in the local community, communicating with professionals who work in the field, and so forth.

After the teacher has created the project, he or she can evaluate its effectiveness before presenting it to the class using the evaluation form shown in Figure 4.3. The purpose of this checklist is to help teachers to become "reflective practitioners."

Step 3.   Next, the teacher should present the problem to his or her students. Several techniques can be used to do this (see Chapter 3). One technique is simulation (role playing), in which students encounter situations similar to those that professionals deal with daily. Other techniques are the inquiry contract, in

Figure 4.3   Problem-Based Learning Activity Evaluation Form

General Information

Title and Source: _____

General Description: _____

Standards Addressed

Math: _____

Science: _____

Technology: _____

Approximate Time Frame: _____

Instruction Criteria Continuum	Excellent		Adequate		Weak	Point Total
Affect						
• Captures student interest	5	4	3	2	1	
• Has meaning and relevancy	5	4	3	2	1	
Content						
• Is developmentally appropriate	5	4	3	2	1	
• Elicits higher-level thinking skills	5	4	3	2	1	
• Engages students in original and creative thinking	5	4	3	2	1	
• Involves research directly from authentic sources	5	4	3	2	1	
• Elicits student interpretation and conjecture	5	4	3	2	1	
Pedagogy						
• Has clear goals and objectives	5	4	3	2	1	
• Has multiple solution possibilities	5	4	3	2	1	
• Elicits the generation of multiple strategies	5	4	3	2	1	
• Promotes inquiry	5	4	3	2	1	
• Elicits student explanations	5	4	3	2	1	
Comments:				Total Project Score: _____		

which the parameters of the problem are set up and discussed, and the case study, in which students are presented with the problem and are asked to deal with it as if they were professionally involved. Workshops and study questions are also options. Depending on the technique used, problem presentation can include teachers reading the problem aloud to students or having students read and discuss a written summary outlining the specifics of the problem situation with their partners or teams.

Step 4.   After the problem presentation, students can begin their research. Teachers can help students get started by providing them with a list of appropriate Web sites or other research sources that could prove to be a helpful starting point. Once the teacher has set students on their course, students are on their own to conduct their research, plan their strategies, form their hypotheses, and find their solutions. During this time the teacher continually circulates and makes him- or herself available to students, periodically asking questions designed to help keep students on track but not offering so much information as to lead the inquiry.

QUESTIONS TO PROMOTE PROBLEM SOLVING

No matter how well designed a PBL project might be, times may arise during the project when students are unsure of how to start or continue the work needed to reach a solution. In this case, they may look to the teacher for help. While teachers want to avoid providing students with answers or directions, they can use various analytic strategies to encourage students to use problem-solving skills. These strategies include the following:

- Recalling and observing evidence related to the problem
- Comparing and clarifying evidence according to predetermined criteria
- Defining the evidence so that it is clear and unambiguous
- Interpreting the data to explain its meaning and significance
- Generalizing from the evidence to derive a principal or main idea
- Inferring from the evidence to predict and hypothesize beyond the data

Teachers can ask students many types of questions to prompt use of these strategies. When students need help understanding, defining, formulating, or explaining the task they are working on, teachers can ask students questions such as the following:

- What do you need to do in order to complete this task?
- What can you tell me about this task that I don't already know?
- How would you interpret that information?
- Could you explain this information in your own words?
- Is there information that seems to be missing?

Sometimes students may come to a point in their research where they lose focus or move away from a solution path that is valid. To get students back on track, teachers can ask students questions that help them see where their thinking may have gone off course. For example, teachers might ask questions such as:

- How can you determine whether or not your answer makes sense?
- Is there anything you might have overlooked?
- What made you think that was what you should do?
- Does this raise any questions for you?

When teachers ask such questions, they must make sure they are not revealing any part of the solution through the questions. Good questions demonstrate respect for students' thinking and understanding and are designed to include the students' own words. For example, teachers might ask, "Why do you think (students' own words)?" or "What do you mean by (students' own words)?" These types of questions require students to make their thoughts and meanings explicit.

Some of the types of questions teachers can use to foster problem solving include the following:

- *Open-ended questions.* These questions have more than one possible answer and cannot be answered with a simple "yes" or "no." For example: "What are some of the things that happen when . . . ?" or "What other methods have you . . . ?"

- *Divergent questions.* These questions get students thinking about other paths they can take in their thinking and may be answered in a variety of ways. For example: "What completely different result would occur if . . . ?" or "We have all positive . . . What are some negative . . . ?"

- *Thought-provoking questions.* These questions demand insight and reasoning. They cannot be answered simply, and they require both logic and reflection. For example: "What have I come to know or come to know differently?" or "What would have to happen or be true in order for . . . ?"

- *Clear questions.* These questions focus on specific phenomena. They cannot be answered with vague generalizations, but rather they provide a clear framework for the desired response. For example: "What would happen if . . . ?" or "How would you . . . ?"

- *Focusing questions.* These questions help students to determine outcomes, sequences, similarities and differences, or cause and effect. For example: "What else is different about . . . as opposed to . . . ?"

Teachers can use different types of questions to achieve various purposes during the PBL process. For example, in the scenario described earlier, Ms. Jones decided she would begin the PBL activity by using open-ended questions to get her students thinking about the rationale for surveys. She began with the following question: "What are some methods an ice cream company might use to find out which of their flavors is the most popular?" Later on in the unit she decided to use the following question, which is both divergent and thought provoking, to help her students think about the validity of their results: "What completely different result would occur if the company decided to survey older ice cream eaters instead of young ice cream eaters?" She then used the following focusing questions after her students had completed their research because she wanted them to understand how their results might be used. She asked her students, "If you brought the results of your ice cream survey to the local store, what effect do you think it might have on the flavors of ice cream they order from their distributor? Why do you think this?"

Figure 4.4 provides a list of specific questions teachers can ask students to facilitate various goals in the problem-solving process.

Figure 4.4   Encouraging Reflection in Problem Solving

Teachers can ask students the following questions to help students achieve success with the problem-solving process.

Goal: To help students to comprehend the problem

- What must be done for this task? What can you tell me about it?
- Can you explain it in your own words?
- Is there something that is missing or is there something you can eliminate?

Goal: To get students to organize their approach to the problem

- Where could you find the information you will need to solve this?
- What have you tried so far? What steps did you take?
- What did not work?
- Do you have a system? A plan? A strategy?
- Have you tried tables, charts, lists, diagrams, or other graphics?

Goal: To help students recognize relationships

- What is the relationship of this to that?
- How is it the same? How is it different?
- Can it be broken down into smaller parts? What would those parts be?

Goal: To encourage students to expand their thinking about possible solutions

- Have you tried making a guess?
- Might a different method work as well or better?
- What else have you tried?

Goal: To prompt students to create a hypothesis

- What do you predict will happen?
- How do you feel about your answer?
- What do you think comes next?
- What else would you like to know?

Goal: To encourage students to reflect and self-assess

- What do you need to do next?
- What are your strengths and weaknesses?
- What have you accomplished?
- Was your own group participation appropriate and helpful?

Goal: To prompt students to formulate solutions

- Is that the only possible answer?
- Besides retracing your steps, how can you determine whether or not your answer makes sense?
- Is there anything you might have overlooked?

Goal: To get students to examine results

- What made you think that was what you should do?
- Is there a real-life situation in which this might be used?
- Where else could this strategy be useful?
- Can you make a general rule from this?

The following inquiry project can be used by teachers to engage students in a PBL experience using the case study technique.

INTEGRATED INQUIRY PROJECT, MULTILEVEL: THE MISSISSIPPI DELTA

The following inquiry project came out of a dilemma faced by a particular geographical area. Teachers might modify this unit by finding a dilemma in their own locales. Teachers can use their own communities as a starting point for the creation of a relevant and meaningful problem situation in need of a solution.

This project can be geared to the elementary, middle, or secondary levels depending on the degree of depth and detail the teacher requires for student research as well as the level of mathematics required for the calculations. Teachers can reduce the number of calculations to make the project more suitable for the elementary level by placing the emphasis on the scientific research aspects of this ecological dilemma rather than the mathematical and computational aspects. To do this, teachers could substitute relative math terms such as *a large amount, an amount greater than, an amount less than,* and so forth to provide a more generalized view of the problem.

Note: While students are eager to undertake research using the Internet and often do not ask for or require assistance, the pedagogical challenge for educators is to encourage students to critically evaluate the authority of the information source. Teachers can encourage students to do such evaluation by reviewing the importance of examining information sources critically. It often helps for teachers to stress the importance of both a source's origin (for example, whether it is from an academic institution such as a university or another well-known organization such as the government) and its background (information about a source is usually provided on the source's homepage).

Project Standards (Grades 5–8)

I. Mathematics Content Standards (Adapted From the National Council of Teachers of Mathematics, 2000)

Standard 1: Numbers and Operations

Instructional programs from pre-kindergarten through grade 12 should enable all students to

- Understand numbers, ways of representing numbers, relationships among numbers, and number systems
- Understand the meaning of operations and how they relate to each other
- Compute fluently and make reasonable estimates

Standard 4: Measurement

Instructional programs from pre-kindergarten through grade 12 should enable all students to

- Understand attributes, units, and systems of measurement
- Apply a variety of techniques, tools, and formulas for determining measurements

Standard 5: Data Analysis and Probability

Instructional programs from pre-kindergarten through grade 12 should enable all students to

- Formulate questions that can be addressed with data and collect, organize, and display relevant data to answer them
- Select and use appropriate statistical methods to analyze data
- Develop and evaluate inferences and predictions that are based on data

Standard 6: Problem Solving

Instructional programs from pre-kindergarten through grade 12 should enable all students to

- Build new mathematical knowledge through problem solving
- Solve problems that arise in mathematics and in other contexts
- Apply and adapt a wide variety of strategies to solve problems
- Monitor and reflect on the process of mathematical problem solving

Standard 7: Reasoning and Proof

Instructional programs from pre-kindergarten through grade 12 should enable all students to

- Select and use various types of reasoning and methods of proof

Standard 8: Communication

Instructional programs from pre-kindergarten through grade 12 should enable all students to

- Organize and consolidate their mathematical thinking through communication
- Communicate their mathematical thinking coherently and clearly to peers, teachers, and others
- Analyze and evaluate the mathematical thinking and strategies of others

Standard 9: Connections

Instructional programs from pre-kindergarten through grade 12 should enable all students to

- Recognize and use connections among mathematical ideas
- Understand how mathematical ideas interconnect and build on one another to produce a coherent whole
- Recognize and apply mathematics in contexts outside of mathematics

Standard 10: Representation

Instructional programs from pre-kindergarten through grade 12 should enable all students to

- Use representations to model and interpret physical, social, and mathematical phenomena

II. Science Content Standards (Adapted From the *National Science Education Standards*, 1995)

Content Standard A: Science as Inquiry

Students should develop:

- Abilities necessary to do scientific inquiry
- Understandings about scientific inquiry

Content Standard C: Life Science

Students should develop an understanding of:

- Populations and ecosystems

Content Standard D: Earth and Space

Students should develop an understanding of:

- Energy in the Earth system

Content Standard E: Science and Technology

Students should develop:

- Abilities of technological design
- Understandings about science and technology

Content Standard F: Science in Personal and Social Perspectives

Students should develop an understanding of:

- Science and technology in local, national, and global challenges

Content Standard G: History and Nature of Science

Students should develop an understanding of:

- Science as a human endeavor
- Nature of scientific knowledge
- Historical perspectives

III. Technology Foundation Standards (International Society for Technology in Education [ISTE]) (Adapted From the *National Educational Technology Standards [NETS] Project*, 1998)

Basic Operations and Concepts

- Students demonstrate a sound understanding of the nature and operation of technology systems.
- Students are proficient in the use of technology.

Technology Productivity Tools

- Students use technology tools to enhance learning, increase productivity, and promote creativity.
- Students use productivity tools to collaborate in constructing technology-enhanced models, preparing publications, and producing other creative works.

Technology Communications Tools

- Students use telecommunications to collaborate, publish, and interact with peers, experts, and other audiences.
- Students use a variety of media and formats to communicate information and ideas effectively to multiple audiences.

Technology Research Tools

- Students use technology to locate, evaluate, and collect information from a variety of sources.
- Students use technology tools to process data and report results.
- Students evaluate and select new information resources and technological innovations based on the appropriateness to specific tasks.

Technology Problem-Solving and Decision-Making Tools

- Students use technology resources for solving problems and making informed decisions.
- Students employ technology in the development of strategies for solving problems in the real world.

Project Task

An environmental project for the Mississippi Delta area is presented in Figure 4.5. The class is to divide into groups to research both the pros and cons of the situation and be ready to present a case in defense of one of the positions (either pro or con).

At the middle level, teachers can copy Figure 4.5 and hand it out to students to read and discuss within their groups. Students should read the information and discuss the pros and cons independently of each other. Once the pros and cons have been discussed among the groups, it is a good idea to have some class discussion about the merits and drawbacks regarding the different positions. This also

Figure 4.5   Environmental Project

Read the following and then consider the questions at the end of the reading.

Every spring the rising Mississippi River turns the Mississippi Delta area into a vast, forested sea. It is an annual ritual of high water, as local people call it, and it has been going on for thousands of years. Although the water sometimes rises as much as 30 feet and stays at that level for weeks at a time, locals never use the word *flood,* which would imply an unexpected, disastrous event. To them, the yearly high tide is simply part of the natural rhythm of life in the Lower Delta.

Today, the land is owned by the U.S. Army Corps of Engineers. It sits at ground zero for a series of plans designed by the Corps to drain and control flooding in the Delta area. The two most notable projects are a $62 million plan to dredge and clear more than 100 miles of the Big Sunflower River to reduce flooding and the construction of a $150 million backwater pumping plant along Steele Bayou, which would transfer floodwaters from one section of the delta to another.

While the Army Corps is pushing ahead with the dredging of the Big Sunflower, critics of both plans question whether U.S. taxpayers should have to pay for projects that will benefit only a small number of local landowners while destroying precious natural resources. At stake are thousands of acres of some of the nation's most productive wetlands and bottomland hardwood forests, which include cypress trees more than 1,000 years old, and a languorous river that nurtures what biologists believe is the densest colony of freshwater mussels on the planet.

In 1963, the Corps bulldozed area woodlands to make way for a system of levees, canals, and pumps that were designed to protect the lower delta from interior and backwater flooding. The levees were to shut out the Mississippi River backwater, and the pumps were designed to lift water from the interior delta and discharge it into the Mississippi. The goal was to make more land available for agriculture. The clearing of hundreds of thousands of acres of trees in the 1960s and 1970s—most of which were merely pushed into windrows and burned—was devastating to wildlife. The floods, meanwhile, persisted, and when the price of soybeans fell in the early 1980s, much of the new land created by the Army Corps was abandoned. Today, a wildlife-based economy is emerging in the lower delta, with resorts offering hunting and fishing excursions as well as nonconsumptive recreational opportunities such as hiking and bird watching. Meanwhile, thousands of acres have been voluntarily reforested or enrolled in federal conservation programs. So why is the U.S. Army Corps of Engineers proceeding with its plans?

The Yazoo River pumps and Big Sunflower dredging projects are leftovers from the early 1940s, when Congress authorized the most ambitious flood control program in U.S. history in the Mississippi Delta. These projects are linked with upstream flood control works that have since been completed. Since the overall plan was not finished in the '40s and '50s, the benefits went only to people upriver, and those in the Lower Delta were left out.

Many area residents are for the plan, but those who are opposed to it fear that

- Dredging the Big Sunflower River will destroy valuable ecosystems in the river, cause further erosion of the river banks, and waste taxpayer dollars.
- The dredging project might increase the current levels of both flooding and erosion (according to Army Corps figures, more than 200,000 acres of cleared land in the backwater area flood on average every five years, and some as often as twice a year).
- The project represents a threat to mussel beds that are thousands of years old. A biologist with the U.S. Fish and Wildlife Service in Mississippi notes that the mussel beds in the Big Sunflower River represent the densest accumulation of biomass in the world. As much as 100 pounds of mussels can be found in a square meter of river bottom.

The Corps has altered its plans for the Big Sunflower as a result of negotiations over the past three or four years, but the dredging might still remove an estimated 40 percent of the mussel beds. Tulane University geologist Barry Kohl worries that the project could also release DDT trapped in river sediments, causing more environmental damage downstream. The experts believe that the issue is not whether to have flood control, since some flood control is essential, but where to draw the line.

(Continued)

Figure 4.5 (Continued)

Last fall, the National Wildlife Federation (NWF) determined that the line was violated when the Army Corps, in its plans to dredge the Big Sunflower, violated U.S. law. According to the federal Water Resources Development Act, proposed water projects must have only a negligible impact on wildlife and its habitat and local sponsors must share the costs of the project. In the case of the Big Sunflower, the Corps maintains that its plans are exempt from this 1986 law because the project amounts to nothing more than "maintenance" on a portion of the river that was authorized for dredging by Congress in 1944. The NWF filed a lawsuit against the U.S. government in November 1998 to stop the project. The NWF maintains that flooding problems can be addressed with less expensive approaches, such as conservation easements that would give landowners financial incentives to reforest lands.

Such approaches could lessen the need for another controversial flood control scheme, the Yazoo pump project. This ambitious plan involves building the world's largest pumps, which would lift 10,000 cubic feet of water per second from Steele Bayou and the Big Sunflower into the Yazoo near its meeting point with the Mississippi. The volume is equivalent to the average flow of the Delaware River, and this would be added to the Mississippi's flow during floods.

How many people will benefit from such an expensive project? The Army Corps cannot say for sure, but critics maintain that the number may be as low as a few dozen and that flooding will be reduced, but not eliminated, on these people's land.

As part of its ongoing efforts to protect the nation's wetlands, the NWF, working with Trial Lawyers for Public Justice (TLPJ), has taken the U.S. Army Corps of Engineers to court to stop the Big Sunflower River dredging project. (TLPJ is a national public-interest law firm.) The NWF is also working to persuade the Corps to abandon its Yazoo backwater pumps project.

- What are the two opposing viewpoints presented here?
- How might each position be defended for and against the plan?

helps to make students aware that issues such as these exist and that different opinions can be valid. After the positions have been discussed and students are familiar with the facts, they can begin conducting their research on both positions via the Internet using the Web sites listed under Resources.

Resources

www.nwf.org

The National Wildlife Federation's homepage can provide teachers with many additional PBL project ideas dealing with ecology; it also serves as an excellent jumping-off point for student Internet research on numerous and varied issues involving ecology and conservation.

www.nwf.org/endangered/index.cfm

The National Wildlife Federation's news page contains direct links to current information and articles dealing with endangered species.

www.nwf.org/globalwarming

Contains information about the effects of global warming on various ecosystems and climate solutions.

www.tlpj.org

Contains information on Trial Lawyers for Public Justice. Students can look up current cases and peruse related issues and publications.

5

Evaluating and Assessing Problem-Based Learning

Problem-based learning (PBL) is a brain-compatible methodology for instruction (it provides its own intrinsic motivation), and as such, problem-based assessment must be brain compatible as well. Just as traditional instructional methodologies appear to work in opposition to the brain's natural way of increasing its knowledge base, traditional methods of assessment fail to measure authentic learning, knowledge, or understanding. From a brain-compatible perspective, assessment must be viewed as an ongoing activity in which teachers gather information about student learning in multiple ways.

This can be accomplished when teachers listen, observe, and talk with students; pose questions; and examine student-created work. Such informal means of assessment must be organized to produce a coherent story of student progress to help students make more progress with greater focus and to complement other types of embedded assessments.

To be compatible with brain function, instruction and assessment practices should encourage students to learn through inquiry, discovery, and the search for patterns and connections. Learning through discovery means students search for solutions to problems through diverse strategies suited to various learning styles. Learners must actively participate in their own learning and meaning making while connecting emotionally, physically, and intellectually with the curriculum topic.

PBL evaluation is more than a single event (such as an end-of-unit or end-of-chapter test). It is a complex process that shapes what teachers look for in and find out about student learning. An inquiry product created for an evaluation entails a synthesis that shows a student's level of skill and judgment by showing how he or she has "put it all together."

ALTERNATIVE ASSESSMENTS

The term *alternative assessment* refers to any assessment other than the traditional test-type assessment. Both the National Council of Teachers of Mathematics (NCTM) standards and the National Science Education Standards (NSES) present a vision of assessment that is highly brain compatible in that it is ongoing and carried out in multiple ways. By listening to, observing, and talking with students; by asking students questions to help reveal their reasoning; and by examining students' individual or group written and/or problem-solving work, teachers are able to develop a more accurate picture of what students know and can do. When developed and used in this way, assessments can provide teachers with direct insight into student thinking and reasoning abilities. In addition, assessment becomes a powerful tool to help teachers monitor the effectiveness of their own teaching, judge the utility of the learning tasks, and consider when they should begin new instruction and where they should go with it.

> Authentic assessments replicate the challenges and standards of performance that typically face writers, business people, scientists, community leaders, designers, or historians. These include writing essays and reports, conducting individual and group research, designing proposals and mock-ups, assembling portfolios and so on. (Wiggins, 1989, p. 703)

One of the major forms of alternative assessment is the authentic (performance) assessment. According to Maria Ruiz-Primo and Richard Shavelson (1996) such performance assessments have at least three components: (1) a task that poses a meaningful problem and entails a solution that requires the use of concrete materials that react to the actions taken by the student, (2) a format for the student's response, and (3) a scoring system that involves judging not only the right answer but also how reasonable the process used to carry out the task is. A performance assessment is considered to be authentic when it involves students in tasks that are worthwhile, significant, and meaningful (tasks that take into account that the search for meaning is innate in all humans). Authentic assessments demonstrate to students exactly what it means to do excellent work by making the standards for judging that work explicit.

Authentic assessments are most brain compatible when they emphasize learning and thinking, especially those higher-order thinking skills involved in inquiry and problem solving (Ronis, 2007). Such assessments comprise meaningful tasks that reflect real-life, interdisciplinary challenges; present students with complex, ambiguous, open-ended problems; and integrate students' knowledge and skills. These assessments usually culminate in student products or

Figure 5.1   Components of Quality Learning Assessments

Assessment Structure

- The assessment does not rely on arbitrary or unrealistic time constraints.
- The assessment contains questions or tasks that are known beforehand and are not "secret."
- The assessment involves multiple opportunities for demonstration of growth (that is, portfolios) rather than one-shot, stressful experiences.
- The assessment is done not individually but rather in collaboration with others.
- The assessment allows for a significant degree of student choice.

Intellectual Design Features of Assessment

- The assessment is constructed to direct students toward more sophisticated uses of knowledge and skills (that is, critical thinking skills).
- The assessment is contextualized so that the task is not isolated from the outcome.
- The assessment evaluates thinking processes rather than bits and pieces of isolated information.
- The assessment involves a somewhat ambiguous or messy task and/or problem situation.
- The assessment involves the student's own research or use of knowledge.
- The assessment presents a challenge that emphasizes depth of knowledge and understanding.
- The assessment is designed to be stimulating and educational, so that students can learn from the assessment process as well as the inquiry process.

Evaluation Standards for the Assessment

- The assessment is based on clearly articulated criteria and performance standards rather than a curve or norm.
- The assessment takes the mystery out of success by using performance indicators that allow students to know ahead of time "what excellence looks like."
- The assessment makes metacognitive activities such as self-assessment and self-reflection part of the total assessment process.
- The assessment uses a multifaceted evaluation system rather than a single numerical grade.

Assessment Equity

- The assessment identifies hidden strengths rather than weaknesses.
- The assessment deemphasizes competitive comparisons between students.
- The assessment allows for different learning styles, abilities, and interests.

SOURCE: Adapted from *Brain-Compatible Assessments* by Diane Ronis. © 2007 Corwin Press. Reprinted with permission of Corwin Press, Thousand Oaks, CA.

performances that recognize and value students' multiple intelligences, varied learning styles, and diverse backgrounds.

Quality PBL assessments should incorporate the characteristics shown in Figure 5.1.

Authentic problem-based assessments reflect the student-centered, constructivist learning paradigm. With this assessment model, the teacher's main role is to assist students in taking responsibility for their own learning and to help students become accomplished self-evaluators.

Another important aspect of a successful assessment is reflection. Teachers are not the only ones making daily judgments in the classroom. Students are also making judgments about themselves and their work. PBL assessments should be metacognitive in that they ask the learner to become self-reflective and employ self-assessment as a way of taking control of his or her own learning.

TYPES OF AUTHENTIC ASSESSMENT AND EVALUATION

Several forms of assessment fit the characteristics of quality authentic assessments that teachers can use with their students. These assessments include portfolios, student performances and presentations, and journals. Rubrics and observation checklists are forms of evaluation that have been developed for rating the products of authentic assessments.

The Rubric

> A scoring rubric is one way of communicating clearly articulated standards before, during, and after a unit of study. (Ronis, 2007, p. 35)

For years the test-obsessed society of the United States has relied on machines to attach numbers to large-scale assessments. Assessment models that are able to quantify or qualify the products of problem solving and inquiry learning, however, cannot be scored in the same way as standardized tests. With an inquiry and problem-solving assessment format, people, rather than machines, must take on the job of appraisal and evaluation. This reliance on human evaluators raises questions about the time involved in conducting assessments as well as the reliability and consistency of assessments based on human judgment. In an effort to manage these concerns, alternative methods for evaluation, such as the rubric, have been developed to go along with these innovative assessments.

A *rubric* is an established set of criteria used for evaluating or rating student products and performances. (Some of the products and performances the rubric can be used with are discussed in the following sections of the chapter.) A rubric describes the levels of performance a student might be expected to attain relative to a desired standard of achievement. These performance descriptions tell the evaluator what qualities to look for in a student's work and how to place that work on a predetermined scale or continuum. Thus, these guidelines make the assessment process faster as well as more consistent. The rubric must be designed (preferably with students), articulated, and modeled prior to the start of the problem inquiry.

Designing a rubric with the class incorporates brain-compatible learning methods into the assessment practice in that it allows students to have a hand in creating their own guidelines and benchmarks for assessment. However, when discussing a rubric with students, it is best if teachers have a general idea as to the standards and criteria they have in mind for the unit so they can help guide the students when the assessment qualities are being discussed and selected.

The following steps can be used as guidelines for developing rubrics with students.

Step 1. The teacher begins the rubric design by first reviewing samples of what the completed project will look like (perhaps using examples saved from previous years or teacher-made samples).

Step 2. The class discusses what constitutes excellence in a project, which is characterized as the Advanced (exemplary) level, and also discusses characteristics of the three other descriptor levels: Proficient (accomplished), Basic (developing), and Novice (beginning).

Step 3. Next the teacher, together with the students, selects the set of criteria that constitutes a valid evaluation. For example, for the PBL project discussed in the example of Ms. Jones's class in Chapter 4, the class would need to decide upon qualities that make a student's graph a high-quality one, such as accuracy, legibility, consistency, and so forth.

Step 4. Once the qualities or characteristics have been chosen, each of those characteristics must be described for each of the four levels. For example, for the Ms. Jones's class project, the characteristic of accuracy could be described for each level as follows:

- *Advanced (exemplary):* All required as well as any additional optional graph entries are recorded with total accuracy.
- *Proficient (accomplished):* All required graph entries are recorded with total accuracy (but only required information is included).
- *Basic (developing):* For the most part, the entries are recorded with a high degree of accuracy (no more than three errors).
- *Novice (beginning):* The entries have a high level of inaccuracy (more than four errors).

Step 5. The teacher synthesizes the criteria and descriptor levels into a draft rubric to show to the class the following day.

Step 6. The teacher and the students polish and refine the rubric in class.

The characteristics of various levels of performance in an inquiry experience are demonstrated in Figure 5.2. The figure starts with characteristics of a successful inquiry experience and ends with characteristics of an inquiry experience that needs to be improved upon. Teachers and students may want to keep these characteristics in mind when creating a rubric for their inquiry project.

Rubric scales may also be based on a numerical continuum, with numbers such as 0 to 4 or 1 to 5 being assigned to the differing levels of achievement. Rubrics are effective because they allow the desired standard of achievement to be clearly communicated. Rubrics help create evaluation systems that are easy to learn and understand. They help students assess their place on the achievement scale and indicate what is necessary to improve their performance. The same rubric can be used repeatedly throughout the year with a multitude of projects to document a pattern of performance and progress. The rubric in Figure 5.3 is an example of a four-level rubric that defines levels of success for aspects of the PBL experience.

Figure 5.2   Characteristics of Various Levels of Success for Inquiry Assessments

---

Advanced (Extended/Sophisticated)

- Is able to make new generalizations from prior experience
- Successfully experiments to create multiple solution paths
- Sophisticated, complex, and detailed explanation of inquiry process and the strategies used

Proficient (Satisfactory/Adequate)

- Demonstrates good comprehension of problem situation
- Able to create a successful strategy or solution path
- Able to describe the inquiry process and strategy used

Basic (Elementary/Partial)

- Demonstrates some awareness and comprehension of problem situation
- Weak, disorganized explanation of strategy or solution path
- Incorrect or inadequate description of the inquiry process or strategy used

Novice (Beginning/Minimal)

- Demonstrates limited awareness and poor assessment of problem situation
- Inadequate and disorganized approach to problem situation
- No clear strategy or inquiry plan

SOURCE: Adapted from rubric in *Brain-Compatible Assessments* by Diane Ronis. © 2000 Corwin Press. Reprinted with permission of Corwin Press.

Figure 5.3   Problem-Based Learning Evaluation Rubric

Criteria	Novice = 1	Basic = 2	Proficient = 3	Advanced = 4
Research quality	Numerous inaccuracies with little if any detail	Inconsistent accuracy but some level of detail	Accurate and competent with relevant detail	Highly accurate and sophisticated with explicit detail
Strategies used	At least one acceptable strategy attempted	At least one acceptable strategy correctly applied	Several high-quality strategies applied	Numerous complex and sophisticated strategies applied
Organization of research	Confusing and clumsy organization	Simple but acceptable organization	Reflective organization demonstrates solid planning	Intuitive organization displays complex and perceptive thinking
Communication	Ineffective and vague	Superficial quality may lead to some confusion	Competent and effective communication	Precise and nuanced communication shows high level of sophistication
Comprehension	Little if any understanding demonstrated	Limited, superficial understanding demonstrated	Demonstrations of accurate and thoughtful understanding	Numerous demonstrations of profound and perceptive understandings
Collaboration	Little evidence of collaboration	Intermittent displays of collaboration	Thoughtful collaboration demonstrated	Highly effective and synergistic collaboration

Rubrics are often supplemented with benchmarks, or performance samples, that serve as concrete standards against which other samples may be judged. Benchmarks are specific examples of previously completed student work (student projects such as graphs, posters, charts) that demonstrate what each of the levels looks like. (For example, a student sample of a graph would be provided at the advanced level, at the proficient level, and so on.) These examples serve as guidelines for students to use when measuring their own work and allow students and teachers to match the new student work to the previously selected examples. Benchmark exemplars help make evaluations more consistent, valid, reliable, and less subjective.

Benchmark Exemplars

In the real world, individuals working as professionals must know the goals and the standards they are expected to meet before beginning a task. For example, all architects know any building they design must be of sound construction. In a real problem, the task may be poorly structured but it is still well defined: the goal is known and understood, but the path to that goal may not be obvious. Students need to be provided with the evaluation criteria and models of excellent performance or production (*benchmark exemplars*) as part of the instruction (not unlike competition judges, who are supplied with similar information when judging sporting events). Students need to know what mastery of the task looks like before beginning the task.

Teachers are often not accustomed to designing a PBL assessment or have not previously been asked to be especially clear about their goals for learning activities. They are used to focusing on activities that engage students. They tend to think of what they're going to do rather than what the result will be. When teaching PBL, teachers must learn to plan backward from the problem goals and objectives. They should start by envisioning the goals and objectives of a PBL exercise and plan the rest of the project after deciding upon these criteria. When planning, teachers need to focus on answering questions such as, "What do I want students to know and be able to do, and how well do they need to do it?" and "What does quality look like?"

A good PBL assessment system includes (1) content standards: what students should know and be able to do, (2) a process for developing assessments for each standard, (3) assessment tasks requiring demonstration of authentic and contextual behavior, and (4) a clearly defined scoring rubric for each of the task assessments.

A high school mathematics teacher kept these characteristics in mind when he created a geometric PBL activity for his class. Mr. Hansen wanted his students to compare and contrast geometric shapes within architectural designs in existing buildings. He wanted his students to have visual experiences and class discussions before beginning the creative aspect of the unit, which was to have students design and build their own original structure models. Mr. Hansen started by selecting the project's content standards, which for this project unit were the following:

Standard 3: Geometry

Instructional programs from pre-kindergarten through grade 12 should enable all students to

- Analyze characteristics and properties of two- and three-dimensional geometric objects and develop arguments about relationships
- Use visualization, spatial reasoning, and geometric modeling to solve problems

Standard 4: Measurement

Instructional programs from pre-kindergarten through grade 12 should enable all students to

- Understand attributes, units, and systems of measurement
- Apply a variety of techniques, tools, and formulas for determining measurements

Standard 6: Problem Solving

Instructional programs from pre-kindergarten through grade 12 should enable all students to

- Build mathematical knowledge through problem solving
- Apply and adopt a wide variety of strategies to solve problems
- Monitor and reflect on the process of mathematical problem solving

Standard 9: Connections

Instructional programs from pre-kindergarten through grade 12 should enable all students to

- Recognize and apply mathematics in contexts outside of mathematics

After identifying the content standards, Mr. Hansen developed the assessment rubric with the class by identifying those characteristics that would clearly demonstrate the learning that had taken place. The class rubric included several charactcristics of a successful project that aligned with the standards selected, such as the following:

- Model employs a variety of geometric forms in its design.
- Plans for model employ accurate measurements and use of scale.
- Project journal demonstrates a workable strategy for the design and construction of the model, an evolving comprehension of geometry in the real world, and insight into the learning process.

Thus, using the characteristics of successful assessment, Mr. Hansen was able to develop an applicable rubric with his class.

Self-Evaluation Rubrics

Self-evaluation rubrics are another important aspect of a good assessment plan. These rubrics differ from self-reflection in that they are more concrete.

A *self-evaluation* rubric often involves having students give themselves a grade for the work done, while a *self-reflection* involves students thinking about their learning and trying to make connections to prior learnings or to find new insights. Figures 5.4–5.6 show self-evaluation rubrics teachers can use with various levels of students. These figures demonstrate sample questions that can be used to help guide students in writing their problem-solving and inquiry reflections. Students can use these rubrics to self-evaluate their work to gauge whether or not they are on the right track. These rubrics can be tailored to fit groups or individuals.

The benefits of using rubrics are numerous for students, teachers, and parents. Learners are empowered to achieve success when they know the guidelines of the rubric before they begin a task. Because they clearly understand what is expected, they can strive to meet or exceed expectations. Students develop enhanced cognitive (knowledge-based) and metacognitive (introspective)

Figure 5.4　Math/Science Report Rubric

Criteria	Novice	Basic	Proficient	Advanced
Introduction	Simplistic and underdeveloped	Uneven development	Well developed	Inventive yet concise
Research quality	Incomplete Does not address many important questions	Uneven Not all questions answered satisfactorily	Competent Answers all questions	Rigorous All questions thoroughly documented
Problem or query	Addresses an issue, but that issue is unrelated to the research topic	Addresses an issue somewhat related to the research topic	Addresses topic issue directly through the research findings	Perceptively addresses topic issue directly through rigorous research findings
Sequence and procedures	Incomplete with many steps out of order or absent	Most of the steps are listed in sequence, with only one or two out of order	Steps are presented in a complete, clear, and logical manner	Steps are elegantly laid out in a sophisticated manner
Data and results	Data table and graph are incomplete and contain inaccuracies	Data table and graph are complete, but inaccuracies are evident	Data table and graph are complete and accurate	Data table and graph are complex, explicit, and precise
Summary and conclusion	Does not address any of the questions	Addresses questions, but conclusions are flawed	Satisfactorily addresses and answers questions	Explicitly addresses all questions with complex and sophisticated conclusions
Grammar and spelling	Frequent errors in spelling and/or grammar	3–5 errors in spelling and/or grammar	No more than two errors throughout report	No errors in grammar or spelling
Appearance	Writing is difficult to read Not all pages are secure Lacking illustration	Most writing is legible with attempted illustrations	Writing is neat and legible, bound in a report cover with illustrations	Neatly typed and bound in a report cover with original illustrations

Figure 5.5   Characteristics of Various Levels of Success for Inquiry Assessments

Name: Date:

Self-Assessment for Group Work

- Were all project objectives and criteria met?

- Were the parts done correctly and accurately?

- Were all written aspects of this project done well (correct spelling and sentence structure, neat and organized)?

Superior: (E)	Satisfactory: (S)	Need for Improvement: (N)
My work is superior/excellent. I made many positive contributions to the team effort. I encouraged other team members and gave them assistance when they needed help. I was instrumental to my team's success.	My work was complete, correct, and accurate. I made some positive contributions to the team effort. I encouraged at least one team member. I helped my team to succeed.	I could have done better. I did not encourage others. I did not worry about my team. I didn't really contribute much to the team effort.

Explain the reasons for the grade you gave yourself in four or five complete sentences. Which team members were most helpful? Which were not?

What new concepts did you learn from doing this project?

Did you find any part of this project difficult? If so, which part?

Was there any part of the project you liked best? Why did you like that part?

What did you enjoy or not enjoy about working with your teammates during this particular project?

How do you feel about the class right now?

What do you think we can do to improve this class?

Figure 5.6   Secondary-Level Problem Reflection Guide

Understanding the Problem Situation

Explain the problem situation in your own words.

What information is missing? Has unnecessary information been given?

What assumptions can you make about this particular problem situation?

Planning the Solution Strategy (Strategies)

How would you explain your strategy plan to another person?

What ideas have you tried so far?

How have you organized your information and why did you organize it in this manner?

How might this problem situation be broken down into smaller components?

Executing the Strategy (Strategies)

Explain how you did the work.

Why did you need to use graphs, tables, charts, or other graphics?

Why did you organize your graphs, tables, charts, and so on, in this manner?

How do you know whether or not your solution will work?

Review of the Work

Is your solution reasonable? What makes you sure of this?

Could you have solved this problem differently? In what way?

What made you decide to use this particular strategy?

Communication

Could you state the problem situation differently?

Can you explain what you are doing and how you are doing it?

How would you explain what you are doing to a teammate who is confused?

Connections

Have you ever solved a problem similar to this one?

In what ways is this one the same? In what ways is it different?

Self-Assessment

What makes this kind of problem solving easy or difficult for you?

Is there something you might have done differently to make the inquiry process easier? What might that be?

processes using rubrics because the known criteria allow them to self-monitor their work (Ronis, 2007).

Classroom teachers are beginning to recognize the value of using rubrics as instructional tools. When the rubric is given prior to the task, the quality of the resultant work increases significantly. In addition to improved student achievement, teachers benefit from fewer misunderstandings about how students are being evaluated. Many parents express strong support for instructional rubrics because they see positive influences on the quality of their children's products and performances. Parents of young children are particularly pleased with the use of rubrics for project tasks, since they can use them to help their children understand and meet the teacher's specific expectations. The challenge for teachers is to use rubrics instructionally to help students understand and apply evaluative criteria to improve their performances.

Rubrics are useful for evaluating more than student products and performances. Rubrics can be also be used by teachers to evaluate projects or ideas they develop themselves (see Figure 4.3 in Chapter 4).

Observation Checklists

Observation checklists can be used in a similar fashion to rubrics in that they measure a student's ability to perform a desired task successfully. Observation checklists can take many forms, but for PBL projects they are most useful when they consist of lists of desired skills teachers want students to gain from completing a project (see Figure 5.7). In this case, students would check

Figure 5.7   Performance Task Observation Checklist for Early Elementary Grades

Was my part of the group budget plan accurate and correct?		
YES	MAYBE	NO
Was I helpful to team members during the project when they needed help?		
YES	MAYBE	NO
Are all my numbers on the money poster correct and in the right order?		
YES	MAYBE	NO
Is my purchasing research work correct? Does it make sense?		
YES	MAYBE	NO
Can I now plan a shopping trip by myself? Can I work with a budget?		
YES	MAYBE	NO

SOURCE: From *Brain-Compatible Mathematics* by Diane Ronis. © 2006 Corwin Press. Reprinted with permission of Corwin Press, Thousand Oaks, CA, www.corwinpress.com. Reproduction authorized only for the local school site or nonprofit organization that has purchased this book.

off a category to ascertain the level to which they achieved the skill. Teachers can create individual observation checklists or group observation checklists to use with students. Observation checklists are useful in assessing PBL projects because teachers can give students a checklist outlining what types of things they are looking for in a successful PBL project. Students should be made aware of such criteria prior to the start of a PBL activity. Once students have this information, they can work toward achieving these goals.

Portfolios

Most people think of the student portfolio as a collection of work that represents a student's progress in a given area. The portfolio, however, is both a product and a process. As a product it is an organized, purposeful collection of documents, artifacts, records of achievement, and reflections. It is a process because documents and experiences are gathered, organized, and used to demonstrate learning and instruction. Some of the basic purposes of portfolios at the elementary and middle levels are the following:

- To show a student's progress and growth over time
- To prove that significant learning is occurring through evidence that addresses growth and development across the curriculum
- To enable parents to see and value their children's progress
- To help parents become partners in their children's education and become more aware of the curriculum their children learn
- To enable the teacher to become more knowledgeable about each student's individual strengths and weaknesses
- To value process, not just products

At the secondary level, the portfolio becomes a showcase of a student's best work, a demonstration of what he or she is capable of achieving.

The portfolio experience revolutionizes current assessment models in that students monitor their own learning. It is through this monitoring that the process of evaluation becomes internalized. This internalization of the self-evaluation process is one of the most important life skills to be learned. One of the purposes of evaluation is to have students become self-evaluating. If students leave school still dependent upon others to tell them when they are adequate, good, or excellent, then educators have missed the whole point of what education is about.

A portfolio may consist of a binder holding an assortment of materials, or it may be a computer disk or CD containing text, audio, and visual files. The portfolio serves as an excellent evaluation tool for the assessment of a PBL project because it not only reflects the brain-compatible learning strategies through which students illustrate their multiple intelligences, but also affords students the opportunity to demonstrate growth and progress. Most teachers who conduct several PBL activities over the course of the school year choose to use a portfolio assessment system as part of their regular evaluation program. Portfolios are often evaluated through specific rubrics (see Figure 5.8) designed for the portfolio evaluation system.

Figure 5.8   Portfolio Evaluation Rubric

Criteria	Novice	Basic	Proficient	Advanced
Presentation	Clumsy and ineffective	Simple	Competent	Sophisticated and elegant
Variety	Little if any variety of evidence	Limited selection of artifacts	Satisfactory selection of artifacts	Contains a wide variety of revealing artifacts
Organization	Weak	Superficial	Effective	Perceptive and complex
Communication	Vague and confusing	Uneven	Clear and complete	Masterful and precise
Evidence of understanding	Artifacts display confusion and/or weak levels of understanding	Artifacts display areas of understanding as well as areas of confusion	Artifacts reveal clear understanding	Artifacts reveal nuanced and complex understanding
Self-assessment	Self-assessment does not correspond to performance	Evidence of some realistic self-assessment	Evidence of reflective self-assessment	Evidence of penetrating and intuitive self-assessment

Figure 5.9   Group Project Presentation Rubric

Criteria	Novice	Basic	Proficient	Advanced
Organization • **Format** • **Transitions**	• Confusing format • Clumsy transitions	• Uneven format • Weak transitions	• Effective format • Competent transitions	• Inventive format • Sophisticated transitions
Teamwork • **Cooperation** • **Synergy**	• Little if any cooperation evident • No synergy exhibited	• Cooperation evident in place • No synergy exhibited	• Satisfactory cooperation • Some synergy evident	• Perceptive cooperation • Elegant synergy (students supported each others' contributions)
Content • **Accuracy** • **Detail**	• Numerous inaccuracies evident • Details missing or incomplete	• Uneven degree of accuracy • Superficial attention to detail	• Competent level of accuracy • Satisfactory attention to detail	• Precise accuracy in all information • Rigorous attention to detail
Presentation • **Sensitivity to audience** • **Style**	• Ignores audience attention throughout presentation • Clumsy and ineffective presentation style	• Aware of audience at times • Simple presentation style	• Demonstrates awareness of audience • Presentation style is effective	• Perceptive attention to audience throughout presentation • Presentation style is sophisticated and elegant

Student Performances and Presentations

A good culminating component for a PBL activity is to have students present their projects to the class in the form of a presentation. In such a presentation, the student team talks about their project, and demonstrates what it does, how it works, what it means, and so forth. The class, as well as the teacher, can then evaluate the presentation using a specific rubric (see Figure 5.9) as a guide.

Journals

A journal is the student's personal written record of observations and reflections. These writings, by their very nature, are subjective. A journal can be used to record thoughts, questions, feelings, summaries, and so forth. Teachers can ask students to use journals to record their work, procedures used, outlines created, predictions made, and thoughts during the PBL process (such as accuracy of predictions made as well as reasons for the results). Students can describe the actual research they have undertaken for the problem solution, as well as each of the steps they used in the process.

The best way for teachers to assess journal writing is through the use of a journal rubric. A rubric is necessary so that students understand from the outset exactly which aspect or components they are being evaluated on (that is, are the journals to concentrate on accurate observations and records or predictions and personal thoughts about the subject area content?). In addition, journal rubrics (see Figure 5.10) help keep the grading as objective as possible by providing parameters for each of the evaluation characteristics.

Figure 5.10   Qualities of a Journal Rubric

Qualities Evaluated	Novice	Basic	Proficient	Advanced
Organization and quality of entries	Beginning level of organization lacking both substantial and relevant entries	Developing basic level of organization as well as quality of entries (uneven)	Accomplished level of organization and quality of entries	Excellent level of organization and superior and unique entries
Description and detail of entries	Entries lack detail in description	Entries display uneven detail and description	Entries display an accomplished level of description and detail	Entries contain a superior level of description and detail
Writing mechanics	Punctuation, grammar, and spelling of poor quality	Erratic punctuation, grammar, and spelling	Accomplished level of punctuation, grammar, and spelling	Excellent writing mechanics (punctuation, grammar, and spelling)
Creativity and sophistication of journal presentation	Journal presentation lacks creativity or sophistication	Some level of creativity observed in journal presentation	Evidence of creativity in presentation	Journal presentation is highly creative and sophisticated

INTEGRATED INQUIRY PROJECT, MULTILEVEL: ARCHITECTURAL DESIGN

The following project lends itself to middle and secondary levels, but it can be easily adapted for the elementary level by providing students with the requisite ecological background material (such as how certain areas come to be classified as wetlands, what the ecological consequences would be if a construction project destroyed a wetlands habitat, and suggestions for avoiding such a project) and by keeping the floor plan designs simple and basic (for example, using the floor plan for a bungalow).

Individual manipulatives such as geoboards (small peg boards used to create geometric shapes by stretching different colored rubber bands around various pegs) can be used to provide hands-on experience for investigations of geometric concepts such as area and perimeter; calculators can be used to extend the development and exploration of pi and area formulas; and computers can be used to furnish a medium for vocabulary work or visual explorations of lines of symmetry and congruency. Each of these enhances geometry instruction according to the goals outlined in the National Council of Teachers of Mathematics (2000) *Standards and Principles for School Mathematics*.

The premise of the Architectural Design collaborative project unit is that students, working for an architectural design firm, must create a house plan for a construction site situated adjacent to an area classified as a wetland. Before beginning their design proposals, students must first learn about wetlands by asking themselves questions such as the following: "What exactly classifies a site as a wetlands area?" "What do wetlands mean for the environment?" "Does the proximity of wetlands to a building site result in any construction restrictions?" Students must take this and other information into account when creating the construction proposal.

An alternative premise teachers can use is to ask students to design a plan for a new inner-city housing project. In this type of situation, students must first research urban decay and redevelopment as well as social and environmental problems brought about by the deterioration of neighborhoods.

Project Standards (Grades 9–12)

I. Mathematics Content Standards

Standard 1: Numbers and Operations

Instructional programs from pre-kindergarten through grade 12 should enable all students to

- Understand numbers, ways of representing numbers, relationships among numbers, and number systems
- Understand the meaning of operations and how they relate to one other
- Compute fluently and make reasonable estimates

Standard 3: Geometry

Instructional programs from pre-kindergarten through grade 12 should enable all students to

- Analyze characteristics and properties of two- and three-dimensional geometric objects and develop arguments about relationships
- Use visualization, spatial reasoning, and geometric modeling to solve problems

Standard 4: Measurement

Instructional programs from pre-kindergarten through grade 12 should enable all students to

- Understand attributes, units, and systems of measurement
- Apply a variety of techniques, tools, and formulas for determining measurements

Standard 6: Problem Solving

Instructional programs from pre-kindergarten through grade 12 should enable all students to

- Build new mathematical knowledge through problem solving
- Solve problems that arise in mathematics and in other contexts
- Apply and adopt a wide variety of strategies to solve problems
- Monitor and reflect on the process of mathematical problem solving

Standard 7: Reasoning and Proof

Instructional programs from pre-kindergarten through grade 12 should enable all students to

- Select and use various types of reasoning and methods of proof

Standard 8: Communication

Instructional programs from pre-kindergarten through grade 12 should enable all students to

- Organize and consolidate their mathematical thinking through communication
- Communicate their mathematical thinking coherently and clearly to peers, teachers, and others
- Analyze and evaluate the mathematical thinking and strategies of others

Standard 9: Connections

Instructional programs from pre-kindergarten through grade 12 should enable all students to

- Recognize and use connections among mathematical ideas
- Understand how mathematical ideas interconnect and build on one another to produce a coherent whole
- Recognize, use, and learn about mathematics in contexts outside of mathematics

Standard 10: Representation

Instructional programs from pre-kindergarten through grade 12 should enable all students to

- Use representations to model and interpret physical, social, and mathematical phenomena

II. Science Content Standards (Adapted From the *National Science Education Standards*, 1995)

Content Standard A: Science as Inquiry

Students should develop:

- Abilities necessary to do scientific inquiry
- Understandings about scientific inquiry

Content Standard C: Life Science

Students should develop an understanding of:

- Populations and ecosystems

Content Standard E: Science and Technology

Students should develop:

- Abilities of technological design
- Understandings about science and technology

Content Standard F: Science in Personal and Social Perspectives

Students should develop an understanding of:

- Science and technology in local, national, and global challenges

Content Standard G: History and Nature of Science

Students should develop an understanding of:

- Nature of scientific knowledge

III. Technology Foundation Standards (International Society for Technology in Education [ISTE]) (Adapted From the *National Educational Technology Standards [NETS] Project*, 1998)

Basic Operations and Concepts

- Students demonstrate a sound understanding of the nature and operation of technology systems.
- Students are proficient in the use of technology.

Technology Productivity Tools

- Students use technology tools to enhance learning, increase productivity, and promote creativity.
- Students use productivity tools to collaborate in constructing technology-enhanced models, preparing publications, and producing other creative works.

Technology Communications Tools

- Students use telecommunications to collaborate, publish, and interact with peers, experts, and other audiences.
- Students use a variety of media and formats to communicate information and ideas effectively to multiple audiences.

Technology Research Tools

- Students use technology to locate, evaluate, and collect information from a variety of sources.

Technology Problem-Solving and Decision-Making Tools

- Students use technology resources for solving problems and making informed decisions.
- Students employ technology in the development of strategies for solving problems in the real world.

Performance Task

Students are to put together a house plan on a lot adjacent to wetlands using the given dimensions and room specifications. Then students should determine the total square footage of their house and how much it will cost to build.

Project Instructions

Teams begin the project by conducting background research for a team report through Internet research about wetlands. As there are numerous sites concerning wetlands (some of which are listed in the Chapter 4 project), students should be able to conduct research to locate sites themselves. Once they have done research, students will be ready to begin the design aspect of the project. Teachers may want to get students thinking about adjusting their design based on the information they found about wetlands by asking students the following questions:

- Do each group's plans include a basement or a crawl space for the house?
- What kind of drainage system (for example, storm drains, dry wells, curtain drains) has been included to handle the excess water on the property?
- If the excess water is to be diverted, where will it be diverted to and why?
- What might be the consequences to local wildlife of decisions about where to divert the water?

Figure 5.11 Sample Perimeter Plan With Calculations

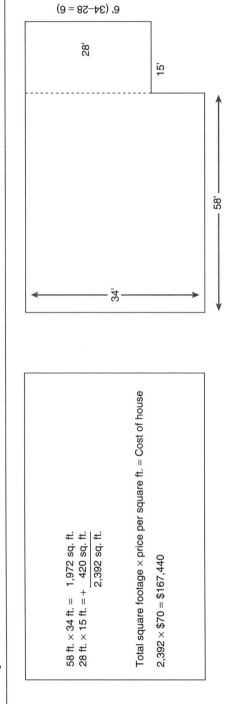

58 ft. × 34 ft. =   1,972 sq. ft.
28 ft. × 15 ft. = +   420 sq. ft.
                       2,392 sq. ft.

Total square footage × price per square ft. = Cost of house

2,392 × $70 = $167,440

6' (34–28 = 6)

28'

15'

58'

34'

Figure 5.12 Sample Floor Plan

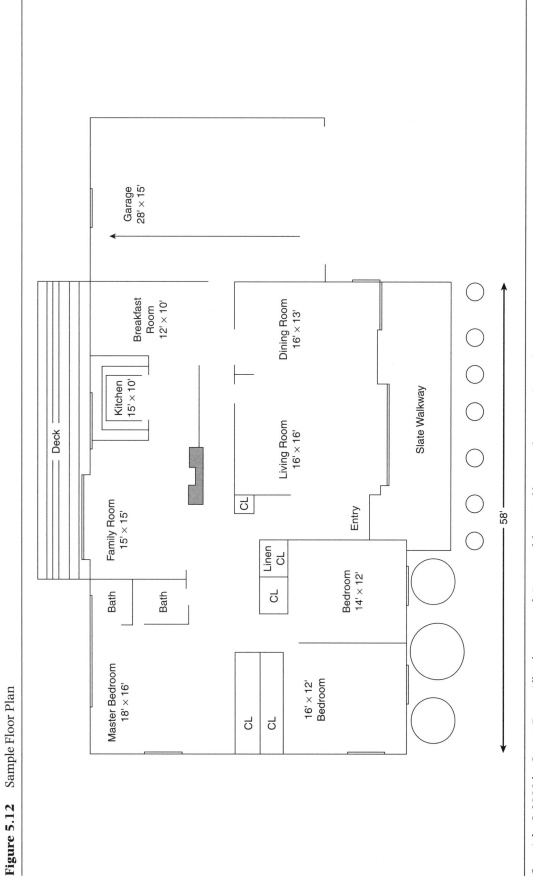

Next, it is a good idea for teachers to help students gain an understanding of floor plans and how to read them by first displaying and discussing examples of floor designs. Teachers can obtain plans from books or magazines at local bookstores or get discarded plans from architects (see Figure 5.11 for an example of a sample perimeter plan). Concepts such as hallways, doors, walls, room sizes, and typical layout designs should all be discussed, as well as square footage and the manner in which the price of a house is determined. Teachers can give students Figure 5.12 as an example of a floor plan. This should be used only as an example, as students are to create their own dimensions.

To help students get an idea of actual room size and proportion, teachers should assign each student the task of measuring various rooms at home, sketching them out on paper, and calculating the square footage of each room. This helps students familiarize themselves with actual room sizes and measurements.

Students are to work in pairs and are given one week in which to design their original floor plans. They are given total freedom in design, but the plan drawing must be drawn to scale (that is, 1/4 in. = 1 sq. ft. or 1 cm = 1 sq. ft.). This requirement provides students with an opportunity to make connections with proportions.

Students should begin to familiarize themselves with blueprint designs by first making rough outlines of their floor plans. This is simply to ensure that the design layouts are logical (for example, they include a kitchen, bathrooms, and closets). At this point, teachers should be circulating while the students work to keep tabs on student progress (for example, correcting possible misconceptions or unworkable ideas such as houses that are too large for the construction site).

After deciding on a floor plan, students must calculate the exact dimensions of their houses and create scale drawings of the design. They must also calculate the square footage of each room as well as the total square footage of the house. The project can be extended to include swimming pools, outdoor hot tubs, and/or patios and decks (the students will need to check Web sites and local pool companies for cost estimates).

Using the cost factor of $70 per square foot, students can determine the approximate cost of building their houses. They can then calculate the cost of financing such a house by checking local banks for interest rates and using both simple and compound interest calculations. They can research different kinds of mortgages, fixed or variable, and discuss the advantages and disadvantages of each kind of loan.

To adapt this project to the secondary level, the additional obstacle of a less-than-ideal building lot should be incorporated. The students then have to research ways of dealing with unevenly sloped property, an existing granite ledge, or property erosion (as in a beach community). This aspect can be connected to a second science unit on the effect local weather hazards (for example, hurricanes, floods, tornadoes, earthquakes) have on construction plans.

Project Evaluation

After students have completed the project, they should measure it against a class-designed rubric and give project presentations in pairs. After the

Figure 5.13   Architectural Design: Self-Assessment

Name: Section: Date:

How to Grade the Floor Plan Design

Plan content and mathematical accuracy: 60%

Were all the measurements calculated completely and correctly?

Were the proportions drawn correctly?

Were the environmental factors taken into consideration?

Creativity and originality: 30%

Was the floor plan original in its conception and design?

Did the plan provide innovative solutions for building site limitations?

Appearance: 10%

Were the house plans neat and well thought out? Were the ruled lines accurate and straight?

In the space below, explain the reasons for the grades you gave yourself in four or five complete sentences. Was your partner helpful? How was or wasn't he/she helpful?

On the back of this sheet, reflect upon the following questions:

1. What new mathematical experiences did this project provide for you?

2. What new ecological concerns did you learn about?

3. Will this come into play in your life outside of school, and if so, how?

presentations have been given, students should assess the project presentations using the class-designed rubric and then do a self-assessment of their project using Figure 5.13. Figure 5.14 shows an example of a class-designed rubric that can be filled out by all members of the class (except for the project presenters) to assess projects. Both of these assessment methods should contribute to the final project grade of each pair.

Figure 5.14   Class Evaluation of Completed Projects and Presentations

Excellent (E)

The house plan is well organized, is easy to understand, and contains some interesting and creative ideas and concepts.

The mathematics are complete, accurate, and carried beyond the basic project requirements.

The environmental concerns are dealt with through a well-conceived plan.

Each partner is well prepared and contributes to the presentation.

The presentation has a clear beginning, middle, and end.

Satisfactory (S)

The presentation is adequate but has nothing especially creative or unique about it.

Most of the mathematics are accurate.

The environmental concerns are taken into consideration.

Both partners contribute something of value.

The presentation makes sense and holds my attention.

Unsatisfactory (U)

The presentation is disorganized and difficult to understand.

The mathematics are incomplete and/or inaccurate.

The environmental concerns are not taken into consideration.

Both partners do not contribute equally.

Explain the reasons for the grade you gave in four or five complete sentences.

6

Integrating Community Learning Activities Into the Classroom

The state of American education began to be questioned in 1983, when the report *A Nation at Risk* was issued by the National Commission on Excellence in Education. Some of the findings of this report were that approximately 23 million American adults were functionally illiterate and that 13 percent of all 17-year-olds could also be considered functionally illiterate. This report resulted in new basics being added to American education, including standards for math, science, social studies, and computer science. These standards were created in response to the fear that if education continued to decline, the United States would lose its competitive edge in the world economy.

In the years since the report was published, concern over improving the quality of education has led to a flurry of activity at the national, state, and local levels. Much of this activity has focused on developing partnerships between schools, businesses, and communities, as the report implied that students needed to be better prepared for entering the workforce. The goal of developing such partnerships is to better prepare students for citizenship and workforce demands.

Partnerships have another benefit as well: weaving the web between school and community integrates civic values as well as learning values into the educational process. Problem-based learning (PBL) helps students understand how they can use what they learn in school outside the classroom.

When this type of learning is combined with a community partnership, the community reaps rewards while at the same time helping students learn how to communicate with various audiences. Thus, the community serves as an ideal setting for PBL.

Many school systems have established service learning activities, which integrate service into the curriculum and/or enable students to earn credit for their involvement in neighborhood nonprofit organizations or service-oriented businesses. For example, service learning takes place when a teacher who is teaching a unit on health encourages students to volunteer at a local clinic or nursing home to broaden their understanding.

In addition to school-based initiatives, there are organizations that deal specifically with the establishment and implementation of community service and business partnership programs. One of the largest such organizations is the National Association of Partners in Education. To find other organizations that do similar work, teachers can search the Internet using the search words "service learning."

THE NATIONAL ASSOCIATION OF PARTNERS IN EDUCATION

The National Association of Partners in Education (NAPE) is one of the primary organizations that has developed school volunteer, intergenerational, community service, and business partnership programs throughout the United States over the past 30 years. The goal of this organization is to improve the academic and personal growth of all children by increasing the number, quality, and scope of effective partnerships; the availability of resources for the formation and support of effective partnerships; and awareness about the importance of partnerships for promoting student success.

Through a grant from the Corporation for National Service, NAPE developed a directory of service-learning and business-education partnerships (check the Web site—http://www.edutopia.org/php/orgs.php?id=ORG_300285/ for more information on obtaining the directory). This directory provides models of exemplary programs and practices for education, business, and community leaders interested in developing business-education partnerships that support service-learning activities to meet the needs of students in local communities.

The following list outlines just a few of the partnership activities of the National Association of Partners in Education and provides links to the homepages of some of those partners and sponsors.

Allstate Foundation

Partners in Education and the Allstate Foundation have developed new training materials—concise, easy-to-use tools for developing school-based partnerships that address violence in schools and how it can be prevented. Materials will be available online for the broadest possible dissemination across the country. This project will encourage greater community involvement to "Keep Our Children Safe" in their homes, schools, and neighborhoods.

AutoZone

Partners in Education works with AutoZone to highlight and support AutoZone Partners in Education programs in stores and schools throughout the United States. AutoZone works closely with schools in local communities to support technical education and overall student success. AutoZone has one of the largest networks of business education partnerships in the United States today.

Corporation for National Service

Partners in Education has been designated a grant-making entity by the Corporation for National Service (http://www.cns.gov). Partners in Education is working with four sites—Orlando, Florida; Chattanooga, Tennessee; Louisville, Kentucky; and Shirley, Arizona—to establish school-based, service-learning, business-education partnership programs or to strengthen existing efforts. Partners in Education provides training and project oversight to these sites for the three-year duration of the project.

ExxonMobil Foundation

Working together for many years, the ExxonMobil Foundation and Partners in Education partnership provides support for the broad range of activities of Partners in Education to strengthen the services available for the field work of the network across the United States. Currently, a major focus of this relationship is the leading-edge research project with Search Institute to document the role of partnerships in providing or enhancing developmental assets that will lead to higher levels of youth success.

McKee Foods

With a longstanding relationship to Partners in Education, McKee Foods is the principal corporate sponsor for the annual National Symposium on Partnerships in Education. This is the premier training and networking conference for business, community, and education leaders. Because of support provided by McKee Foods Corporation, the registration fees for the symposium are kept low, encouraging greater involvement of leaders from across the country at the event. The symposium draws more than 1,500 leaders annually.

Metropolitan Life Foundation

Partners in Education and the Metropolitan Life Foundation have worked together to address many issues and needs for children and families. Most recently, this work included a project that created and published practical training materials on "how to" develop high-quality afterschool programs using partnership as a key strategy in urban, rural, and suburban settings. A national awards program highlighted "best-practice" models to facilitate replication and support the development of new afterschool programs.

SBC Foundation

Partners in Education, in partnership with SBC Foundation, developed a telecommunications technology partnership guide, *Out of the Box and Onto the Web*. The publication focuses on how to integrate telecommunications technology into education using community partnerships as a core strategy. Building on the success of the guide, an exciting new SBC Telecommunications Partnership Awards Program was launched in 2000.

Shell Oil Company Foundation

Partners in Education has worked with Shell Oil Company Foundation to address the needs of youth and schools in the urban areas of our country. This specific focus has led to workshops, trainings, and presentations that explore the unique needs in these areas and best-practice models to facilitate replication.

United States Department of Education

Through a congressional appropriation, Partners in Education is just completing a National Survey on Partnerships in School Districts across the country. This 10-year reflection on education partnerships will provide critically important information on growth and trends and enable the development of a set of broad recommendations that will provide a new policy framework for partnerships as we move into this millennium.

Verizon

A new program was established in 2000 that provides the opportunity for Partners in Education to identify and explore key issues in the field of education partnerships. The Verizon Fellowship generates articles and issue papers that are placed in key education publications and on their Web site to bring new information to the network and advance the knowledge base of the field.

W. K. Kellogg

With funding from the W. K. Kellogg (http://www.wkkf.org) and Johnson foundations, Partners in Education convened a Wingspread Conference at which practitioners from nonprofits, businesses, government, and foundations discussed the expansion of collaborative service-learning and school-to-career activities. Outcomes of this conference were published in a public briefing that outlines strategies and principles for cross-sector school-to-career and service-learning partnerships.

In addition to these partners, which are involved in national projects and programs, Partners in Education has a broad range of support and involvement from other groups. These include:

Atofina

AT&T Foundation

Baker Petrolite

Bank of America

BASF FINA

BellSouth

Booz-Allen & Hamilton

Ceridian Corporation

Charles S. Mott Foundation

Chevron Corporation

Compaq Computer Corporation

Cooper Industries

Discovery Networks

Entergy, Inc.

Equiva Services

Exxon Education Foundation

GE Fund

Hewlett Packard

Home State Bank

Honeywell

Houston Chronicle

Intellectual Development Systems

International Paper (Champion)

Lamson & Sessions

McNair Family Foundation

Mitchell Energy & Development

Pizza Hut, Inc.

Premier School Agendas

Reliant Energy

Target

TRW, Inc.

United Technologies Corporation

USA Today

VALIC/American General Financial

Washington Mutual

National Education Coalitions

In addition to partners and sponsors that provide financial support and other resources, Partners in Education continues to play a leadership role with other national organizations. The association works to promote partnership as a strategy to achieve systemic education reform through coalitions such as the National Business Roundtable's Education Task Force, the Education Leaders Consortium, the National Coalition for Parent Involvement in Education, the National and Community Service Coalition, the National Alliance for Business, Business Coalition for Education Reform (http://www.bcer.org), Coalition for Community Schools, Connect America, Partnership for Family Involvement in Education (http://www.pfie.ed.gov), and the International Partnership Network.

Setting Up Partnerships: NAPE's 12-Step Development Process

All of NAPE's publications and trainings for partnership creation, development, and management are based on its 12-Step Partnership Development Process. Depending on the circumstances of the partnership, the goals of the partnership, and the time and resources available, it may be necessary for teachers to emphasize some steps over others. However, NAPE recommends that developers give thought to all the steps at the outset and refer to them repeatedly during the plan development. This process has been designed to help put together partnerships that are uniquely suited to meet the needs of schools and businesses in different communities.

The steps in the process are the following:

1. *Awareness.* Inform the audience involved that a partnership is being considered as a means of improving the schools and the community.

2. *Needs Assessment.* Gather and interpret the information necessary to formulate the goals and objectives of a partnership.

3. *Potential Resources.* Identify and locate the people, materials, equipment, and funding available within the school, school district, business, and community so as to help meet identified needs.

4. *Goals and Objectives.* Set the goals and objectives for the partnership. (A goal is a broad-based statement of purpose for the partnership. An objective is a statement of intended outcome for the partnership. The objective is measurable, is specific, and determines the focus of evaluation.)

5. *Program Design.* Design specific strategies for achieving the partnership's goals and objectives.

6. *Management.* Establish the partnership's administrative structure and set the rules and regulations under which the partnership will function.

7. *Recruitment.* Engage people, organizations, and resources that are to become involved in the partnership and that will respond to the needs identified by the school and the community. (Recruitment also serves as an ongoing

awareness activity—an opportunity to let people know what the partnership is about.)

8. *Assignment.* Match the people who are interested in the partnership with the jobs that need to be done. (Assignment is also the process of matching financial and material resources to identified needs.)

9. *Orientation.* Begin the process that prepares people for involvement in a new experience and helps them understand their roles, as well as the rules, policies, and procedures.

10. *Training.* Prepare the individuals or groups to perform specific tasks in predetermined situations.

11. *Retention.* Set up a plan to encourage the partners to remain involved through their annual reenlistment. Reenlistment is the key to maintaining a strong, effective partnership, and recognition is one of the major retention strategies (rewarding contributions).

12. *Evaluation.* Monitor and evaluate the plan to collect and interpret data that will be used for decision making and improvement.

NAPE Resources

Teachers can use or adapt the NAPE resources to set up their own models for service learning. Many of these partnerships involve publications teachers may find helpful in organizing a local partnership or project. Teachers can access these publications through the NAPE Web site (http://www.edutopia.org/php/orgs.php?id=ORG_300285/), by writing to NAPE at National Association of Partners in Education, 901 North Pitt Street, Suite 320, Alexandria, VA 22314, or by phone (703-836-4880) or fax (703-836-6941). Following is information on several publications teachers may find helpful.

Integrating Telecommunications Technology Into Education

Education systems must provide today's youth with a set of skills that includes using the current telecommunications technologies as a source of life-long learning and as a basic tool in the workplace. To build such systems, teachers need to ask themselves how business-education partnerships have contributed to the successful integration of telecommunications into systemic reform. They also need to ask how these models can be replicated in their community.

The publication *Integrating Telecommunications Technology into Education* highlights telecommunications partnerships that are revolutionizing the way teaching and learning are taking place in classrooms across the country. Analysis of these models discusses the process used for building partnerships that has resulted in the transformation of education. Examples demonstrate how awareness was created in potential stakeholders, how goals and objectives were developed, how resources were identified, and how evaluation of these partnerships was conducted. By focusing on the partnership development process, this publication provides examples of how collaborative communities related to telecommunications technology can be formed.

Partners in Education Guide

Policymakers, business leaders, and educators have recognized telecommunications and technology skills as "the new basics" in education. The federal Technology Literacy Challenge encourages all sectors of society to work as partners to ensure that all children have the opportunity to obtain these skills. The *Partners in Education Guide* helps educators and other community stakeholders learn from schools and communities that are successfully engaging in partnerships in technology. This guide provides an overview of:

- Why it is important to integrate telecommunications technology into education
- How to develop a partnership that facilitates the integration of technology into schools
- What has happened as a result of telecommunications technology integration into education

Complete with model programs and resources, this guide helps educators develop and/or implement a telecommunications technology partnership.

Developing Community Partnerships for School-to-Career Systems

All students need to understand how what they learn in school applies to real-life situations, including the world of work. The creation of an effective school-to-career system that engages community stakeholders in partnerships assists students in experiencing that connection. The manual *Developing Community Partnerships for School-to-Career Systems* provides facilitation methods and other tools teachers can use to create and strengthen the partnerships necessary to create a school-to-career system that best serves the needs of students as they make the transition from school to postsecondary education or work. Relationships in the school-to-career system most often take the form of "mentorships," in which a student or group of students interested in a certain career are teamed with a career professional who gives them information and background on the career. Teachers can initiate such partnerships by contacting businesses or even individuals in the field who might be interested in becoming mentors. One of the features of this publication is a self-instructional guide for educators that explains how to take a work-based experience and turn it into meaningful lessons and curricular units.

A Guide for Evaluating Partnerships: Assessing the Impact of Employee, Parent, Family, and Community Involvement in Education

The goal of community involvement in education is to better prepare students for citizenship and workforce demands. But are these partnerships working?

Many claims have been made about the value of partnerships for improving student outcomes and achieving systemic change for education. While these claims may be accurate, the fact remains that little research is available to substantiate the contribution of partnerships to these broad goals. How can partnership success be measured?

A guide created by NAPE answers such questions. *A Guide for Evaluating Partnerships: Assessing the Impact of Employee, Parent, Family, and Community Involvement in Education* provides partnership participants with information for designing and conducting evaluation activities to determine the effectiveness of individual initiatives.

ORGANIZATIONAL PARTNERSHIPS IN EDUCATION

In addition to NAPE, many other organizations and companies have formed their own partnerships in education; the information concerning these programs is easily accessible to anyone via the Internet. Following are just a few of the many such offerings.

- *Regional Education Laboratories Internet Resources on Community Partnerships* (http://eric-web.tc.columbia.edu/community/partner.html). This Web site provides links to numerous community-education partnerships across the United States.

- *The Laboratory for Student Success* (http://www.temple.edu/LSS/). The Laboratory for Student Success (LSS) is one of 10 Regional Educational Laboratories (RELs) funded by the Office of Educational Research and Improvement of the U.S. Department of Education. The overarching goal of the LSS is to strengthen the capacity of the mid-Atlantic region—Delaware, Maryland, New Jersey, Pennsylvania, and Washington, D.C.—to enact and sustain lasting systemic educational reform through collaborative programs of applied research and development and services to the field. In particular, LSS seeks to achieve high academic standards in urban schools in the mid-Atlantic region and nationally through a comprehensive program of urban education enhancement.

- *Northeast and Islands Regional Educational Laboratory (LAB) at Brown University* (http://www. alliance.brown/edu). One important component of the LAB's research explores how education can better address the needs of culturally and linguistically diverse populations. As part of its initiatives, the LAB sponsors inquiry into the ways learning standards, portfolio assessment systems, and math and science instructional practices might be revised to more effectively challenge students from these backgrounds. The LAB also places an emphasis on developing community and practitioner leadership in linguistically and culturally diverse educational settings. Within the LAB's Urban Initiative, much of which involves collaboration with multicultural urban schools, the LAB also sponsors specific research into school-to-career strategies in urban settings. Finally, the LAB's inquiry into school change and community involvement works with linguistically and culturally diverse populations to understand both the kinds of interaction between schools and communities and the kinds of structures within schools that support sustained school improvement.

- *Northwest Regional Educational Laboratory (NWREL)* (www.nwrel.org/ecc).
  - o *Out-of-School Time/21st-Century Community Learning Centers.* There is a lot going on after school! Locate links and resources to support out-of-school-time programs, including 21st-Century Community Learning Centers.
  - o *Research and Evaluation.* The Education, Career & Community (ECC) professional staff conduct formative and summative evaluations for schools, organizations, institutions, and more on using research and evaluation to improve programs.
  - o *Youth Development.* Learn about NWREL's wide range of training, technical assistance, professional development, curriculum development, and consultation on youth development, community-based learning, and school-to-work transitions. Connect with publications, resources, and NWREL staff to make your programs with young people even more successful!

- *U.S. Coast Guard Partnership in Education Program* (http://www.uscg.mil/edu/pie/pindex.html). The Coast Guard's Partnership in Education (PIE) program supports the Garrett A. Morgan (GAM) Technology and Transportation Futures program. The GAM program is a new national initiative to stimulate public and private partnerships with educators and to integrate transportation-related learning into each grade level, thereby making math and science relevant to students.

  The Coast Guard's PIE program emphasizes four strategies for effectiveness:

  1. *Quality Achievement:* Improved test scores, increased student interest, and increased school attendance
  2. *Excellence in Education:* Enhanced student learning in reading, math, the sciences, computers, and drug awareness
  3. *Improved Educational Opportunities:* Varied participation in classroom instruction
  4. *Improved Coast Guard Visibility:* To create greater awareness and understanding of the Coast Guard and its roles and missions in today's society

HELPING EXPERTS BECOME TEACHERS

Just as teachers often experience difficulty in adjusting to the role of facilitator, many community experts also experience difficulty when adjusting the role of teacher. When invited to take part in a classroom situation, community experts often do a good job of relating to students but may not employ strategies fundamental to good teaching. Strategies they often overlook can be as basic as the use of thought-provoking questions to engage students in active discussion, or simply providing enough time for students to process and reflect upon the information offered before moving on to additional and perhaps more complex information. Although community experts may be effective in their jobs, they may need some guidance to help them become better teachers. Therefore, it is important that community experts first understand the educational philosophy that underpins inquiry learning. They need to know they are not going to be lecturing students but rather sharing information and helping students learn how to search for information.

Community experts also need to be made aware that students will ask some questions they won't be able to answer, and that when this occurs, it is not necessarily a bad thing. While students may initially be nervous that they won't be viewed as bright because they have questions, professionals are often equally concerned that they won't be considered knowledgeable if they can't answer certain questions. Teachers should help community experts understand that the search for information is what is crucial to this kind of learning experience, not the answers students give. Students often don't have the correct answers, and errors and inaccuracies in problem solving typically occur as students go through the process. The important part of the process for students is determining why such errors occurred.

Teachers can make sure community experts are aware of the framework of the PBL experience by contacting the expert before he or she visits the class. Such contact can take the form of a phone conversation or even a short meeting prior to the classroom visit. It is during this PBL orientation that the teacher explains the characteristics of PBL and the inquiry process as well as the kinds of information that would be most helpful to the students.

Once community experts understand the PBL philosophy, teachers can help them improve their instructional strategies. One of the ways teachers can facilitate this process is by providing community experts with a list of lesson objectives. Community experts involved with PBL need to know that one of the objectives is to have students study the learning issues and generate some hypotheses about the issues. Teachers should stress that the way in which community experts can be most helpful is by guiding students in forming hypotheses, not just in getting correct answers.

Teachers also need to share their tips on how community experts can structure group work in the classroom. Community experts need to understand that it's helpful to give each student in the group a specific responsibility. For example, they might ask one student to keep track of the data, another student to run a test, and another to generate a preliminary hypothesis. This structure ensures that everyone is working on the problem. While the community expert may maintain the discourse, it is the teacher's job to be involved and present as a moderator in case he or she is needed to answer questions or offer suggestions.

While this "teacher training" may initially require additional time on the part of teachers, such training and preparation of community experts is a worthwhile investment for several reasons. When community experts are asked to help teach students, schools strengthen their ties to surrounding neighborhoods, and students see firsthand how what they learn in school is used on the job. For example, students can learn how a real estate agent or a car dealer uses math for financial estimations and calculations.

Community experts who act as facilitators are also role models for students. Students develop friendships with these professionals and often make career choices based on some of these associations. This allows students to recognize that school is worthwhile, and that they are just as capable of pursuing careers as the people from whom they are learning.

The community serves as a rich resource for learning about authentic problems and how people outside the classroom search for what they need in their work and in their personal lives. The following inquiry research project is an interdisciplinary unit involving research, analysis, hypotheses, and conclusions.

COMMUNITY CONNECTIONS: MULTILEVEL CAR PROJECT

The contextual learning in the following project is designed around student interests. All the learning is structured around real issues and problems. The students work together in teams, and the learning takes place outside the classroom as well as inside. Students have the opportunity to monitor as well as maximize their learning. Metacognitive opportunities, which allow for self-reflection and self-monitoring, are also included in the activity.

Teachers can simplify this unit for elementary grades by providing students with parts of the necessary financial data and/or by requiring a less complex analysis of the car mechanisms. For example, teachers can ask students to compare only a limited number of auto specifications, such as fuel economy, engine size, and acceleration rate. In addition, teachers may also wish to limit the number of financing options (for example, use only auto loans at fixed interest rates) to simplify the unit. Teachers can make this unit more complex for the secondary level by requiring more detailed investigations of car performance (for example, asking students to report on gear ratios, synchronization, engine torque, or engine combustion) and data used for analysis and comparisons (use of computer spreadsheet and graphing programs).

Project Standards (Grades 3–12)

I. Mathematics Content Standards (Adapted From the National Council of Teachers of Mathematics, 2000)

Standard 1: Numbers and Operations

Instructional programs from pre-kindergarten through grade 12 should enable all students to

- Understand numbers, ways of representing numbers, relationships among numbers, and number systems
- Understand the meaning of operations and how they relate to one another
- Compute fluently and make reasonable estimates

Standard 4: Measurement

Instructional programs from pre-kindergarten through grade 12 should enable all students to

- Understand attributes, units, and systems of measurement
- Apply a variety of techniques, tools, and formulas for determining measurements

Standard 5: Data Analysis and Probability

Instructional programs from pre-kindergarten through grade 12 should enable all students to

- Formulate questions that can be addressed with data and collect, organize, and display relevant data to answer them
- Develop and evaluate inferences and predictions that are based on data

Standard 6: Problem Solving

Instructional programs from pre-kindergarten through grade 12 should enable all students to

- Build new mathematical knowledge through problem solving
- Solve problems that arise in mathematics and in other contexts
- Apply and adapt a wide variety of strategies to solve problems
- Monitor and reflect on the process of mathematical problem solving

Standard 8: Communication

Instructional programs from pre-kindergarten through grade 12 should enable all students to

- Organize and consolidate their mathematical thinking through communication
- Communicate their mathematical thinking coherently and clearly to peers, teachers, and others
- Analyze and evaluate the mathematical thinking and strategies of others

Standard 9: Connections

Instructional programs from pre-kindergarten through grade 12 should enable all students to

- Recognize and use connections among mathematical ideas
- Understand how mathematical ideas interconnect and build on one another to produce a coherent whole
- Recognize and apply mathematics in contexts outside of mathematics

Standard 10: Representation

Instructional programs from pre-kindergarten through grade 12 should enable all students to

- Create and use representations to organize, record, and communicate mathematical ideas
- Use representations to model and interpret physical, social, and mathematical phenomena

II. Science Content Standards (Adapted From the *National Science Education Standards*, 1995)

Content Standard A: Science as Inquiry

Students should develop:

- Abilities necessary to do scientific inquiry
- Understandings about scientific inquiry

Content Standard B: Physical Science

Students should develop an understanding of:

- Motions and forces

Content Standard E: Science and Technology

Students should develop:

- Abilities of technological design
- Understandings about science and technology

Content Standard F: Science in Personal and Social Perspectives

Students should develop an understanding of:

- Science and technology in local, national, and global challenges

Content Standard G: History and Nature of Science

Students should develop an understanding of:

- Science as a human endeavor
- Nature of scientific knowledge
- Historical perspectives

III. Technology Foundation Standards (International Society for Technology in Education [ISTE]) (Adapted From the *National Educational Technology Standards [NETS] Project*, 1998)

Basic Operations and Concepts

- Students demonstrate a sound understanding of the nature and operation of technology systems.
- Students are proficient in the use of technology.

Social, Ethical, and Human Issues

- Students practice responsible use of technology systems, information, and software.
- Students develop positive attitudes toward technology uses that support lifelong learning, collaboration, personal pursuits, and productivity.

Technology Productivity Tools

- Students use technology tools to enhance learning, increase productivity, and promote creativity.
- Students use productivity tools to collaborate in constructing technology-enhanced models, preparing publications, and producing other creative works.

Technology Communications Tools

- Students use telecommunications to collaborate, publish, and interact with peers, experts, and other audiences.
- Students use a variety of media and formats to communicate information and ideas effectively to multiple audiences.

Technology Research Tools

- Students use technology to locate, evaluate, and collect information from a variety of sources.
- Students use technology tools to process data and report results.
- Students evaluate and select new information resources and technological innovations based on the appropriateness to specific tasks.

Technology Problem-Solving and Decision-Making Tools

- Students use technology resources for solving problems and making informed decisions.
- Students employ technology in the development of strategies for solving problems in the real world.

Performance Task

Each group receives a $4,000 allowance for a down payment on a new car. Each student is to select a car using *Consumer Reports* and sources from the Internet to research selections. Students should list and explain the mechanistic and design reasons for their final selection (there should be no duplication of car choice within groups).

Students are to contact local automotive dealerships by phone, letter, e-mail, or in person to find the best price for the selection (price includes any options they may want, sales tax, and destination or handling charges).

Students should find out what finance and/or leasing terms are available from dealerships, area banks, or other sources through the Internet. Then, students should design a financial plan they would be able to live with (assuming they would "obtain" some part-time work). Students should combine all the information within their group and look for similarities and differences among their car selections and finance plans.

In the next step, students should make a comparison study of their group's choices. Together, group members should write a group report that organizes the information their group will present to the class (all members must take part in the presentation). Students should make inferences, draw conclusions, and then evaluate their choices. Then, they should decide as a group which car was the best choice and why. Students should include comparison graphs and charts to visually explain their car choice comparisons to the class. Students should also include letters of appreciation and/or dissatisfaction for each of the dealerships and banks they used for their research. These letters should be in correct business format and should be done on the word processor.

Presentation Evaluation

The presentation evaluation form shown in Figure 6.1 is to be used by the students when they evaluate each other's presentations. This encourages them to become self-evaluative.

Teachers can use the report rubric shown in Figure 6.2 for evaluation purposes, and students can use this rubric as a guide when preparing the report. Students can use Figure 6.3 to self-evaluate their reports to determine if they are on target.

Figure 6.1   Evaluation for Community Connections: Car Project Presentation

Part 1: Presentation Content

4 = advanced; 3 = proficient; 2 = basic; 1 = novice; total point range: 7–28

Members demonstrate_____knowledge of car selections.

Members demonstrate_____knowledge of financial plans.

Members demonstrate_____level of automotive knowledge.

_____ Level of graphs and/or other visual aids provided during presentation.

Group used a(n)_____level of presentation aids that incorporate technology.

All members were able to answer relevant and appropriate questions at a(n)_____level.

_____ Level of community involvement and cooperation.

Were the critical thinking objectives for this assignment obvious from the presentation?

yes = 4 points; no = 0 points; total point range: 0–24

Comparing and contrasting

_____ Identifying similarities and differences

_____ Classifying and sequencing

_____ Strategy planning

_____ Deductive and inductive reasoning as well as logic

_____ Analyzing, evaluating, synthesizing, and interpreting

Part 2: Presentation Organization

4 = advanced; 3 = proficient; 2 = basic; 1 = novice; total point range: 6–24

_____ Logical, sequential order to presentation

_____ Interesting beginning

_____ Informative middle

_____ Strong conclusion

_____ Well planned (not done "off the cuff")

_____ Interactive presentation (audience involvement)

Part 3: Presentation Skills

4 = exceptional; 2 = average; 0 = poor; total point range: 0–24

_____ Excellent eye contact with entire audience

_____ Clear articulation (speaks clearly)

_____ Clearly audible (easily heard)

_____ Appropriate hand gestures and expressions

_____ Good supportive materials (graphs, charts, diagrams, posters)

_____ Demonstrates confidence

Point Total: _____

Figure 6.2 Community Connections: Car Project Presentation Rubric

Report Title:
Authors:

Criteria	Novice	Basic	Proficient	Advanced
Introduction	Simplistic and dull	Superficial	Well developed	Inventive yet concise
Research quality	Incomplete Does not address many important questions	Uneven Not all questions answered satisfactorily	Competent Answers all questions	Rigorous All questions thoroughly documented
Problem or query	Addresses an issue, but that issue is unrelated to the research topic	Addresses an issue somewhat related to the research topic	Addresses topic issue directly through the research findings	Perceptively addresses topic issue directly through rigorous research findings
Sequence and procedures	Incomplete, with many steps out of order or absent	Most of the steps are listed in sequence with only one or two out of order	Steps are presented in a complete, clear, and logical manner	Steps are elegantly laid out in a profoundly sophisticated manner
Data and results	Data table and graph are incomplete and contain inaccuracies	Data table and graph are complete, but inaccuracies are evident	Data table and graph are complete and accurate	Data table and graph are complex, explicit, and precise
Conclusions	Does not address any of the questions	Addresses questions, but conclusions are flawed	Satisfactorily addresses and answers questions	Explicitly addresses all questions with complex and sophisticated conclusions
Grammar and spelling	Frequent errors in spelling and/or grammar	3–5 errors in spelling and/or grammar	No more than two errors throughout report	No errors in grammar or spelling
Appearance	Writing is difficult to read Not all pages are secure Lacking illustration	Most writing is legible with attempted illustrations	Writing is neat and legible, bound in a report cover with illustrations	Neatly typed and bound in a report cover with original illustrations
Punctuality	Report handed in more than one day after due date	Report handed in one day late	Report handed in on due date	Report handed in before due date

Figure 6.3   Community Connections: Car Project Self-Evaluation and Reflection

Name: _____   Section: _____   Date: _____

Content (60 Points)

- The report must include a detailed explanation of each financial plan.
- Specific engineering and design reasons must be offered in support of the automotive selections.
- The report must include valid comparisons of the different cars as well as a group conclusion as to which selection was best and why.

Graphs, Charts, and Diagrams (30 points)

- A minimum of one graph per group member must be included; the more graphs and/or charts included, the higher the grade.
- The graphs and charts must be easy to understand, accurate, organized well, and neatly drawn.

Appearance (10 points)

- The report must be well written (correct spelling and sentence structure), neat, and organized well.
- The report cover must be attractively done, showing effort and care.

In the area below and on the back of the paper, please explain the reasons for your grading. In addition to the above numerical grade, you are to write a reflection describing your thoughts on the new information you have gained from this project, your research, your conclusions, and your interactions with other group members. How and why do you think you might use this information in the future?

Appendix

CYBER SOURCES FOR MATH, SCIENCE, AND TECHNOLOGY

Problem-based learning (PBL) activities and lessons develop students' problem-solving and decision-making abilities through the use of human and material resources, processes, and technological systems. PBL prepares students for lifelong learning in a technological society because it exposes students to activity-oriented laboratory experiences that reinforce abstract concepts with concrete experiences. This combined "know-how" and the "ability to do" in carrying out technological work transforms technological understandings, communication skills, language arts skills, social and societal understandings, mathematical concepts, and scientific knowledge into realities that students can use.

Internet technology education offers a selection of integrated, experience-based instructional programs designed to prepare students to be knowledgeable about technology and its evolution, systems, utilization, and social and cultural significance. The following Web sites represent a selection of Internet informational sources for math, science, and/or technology. A description of each Web site follows the Web site address. Teachers can first review these Web sites on their own to gather information for their teaching practices or as background information for project unit designs. They can also direct students to these Web sites as part of the student research conducted for PBL projects (or for any assignment needing research information, for that matter). It is beneficial if teachers use Web sites such as these as part of the daily classroom experience to integrate technology and the Internet into their students' education and lives.

- Alliance to Save Energy (www.ase.org/educators)

Alliance to Save Energy is a coalition promoting clean, efficient energy use. This Web site offers elementary-level energy-related curriculum aids such as lesson plans about energy conservation, efficiency, and sources.

The concept of energy efficiency can provide multidisciplinary learning opportunities when students use it as a basis to research the following kinds of PBL activities:

- o Computing energy and monetary savings, and/or pollution emissions (Mathematics)
- o Evaluating and comparing appliance efficiency or the environmental effects of burning fossil fuels (Science)

137

o Reading and analyzing different approaches to energy policies (Language arts)
o Entering data into graphing programs (Computer skills)

- The Annenberg/CPB Channel (www.learner.org/)

The Annenberg/CPB Channel provides free educational programming for schools, colleges, and communities, funded by Annenberg/CPB Projects in association with Harvard University and the Smithsonian Institution.

The channel airs television programs for math and science (K–12), as well as programs from popular PBS series that teach a range of subjects. The channel offers video interviews, computer graphics, case studies, and historical footage to enhance high school and college classes across the curriculum. It also offers professional development programs that provide a window into K–12 classrooms in which teachers are trying new approaches to math and science using hands-on and inquiry learning techniques.

- Epsilon Pi Tau (www.epsilonpitau.org)

This site represents the international society for professions in technology. It is of interest to executives of business and industry; technicians and engineers; teachers in elementary grades through high school; and students, instructors, and professors in higher education.

- Explore the Universe (www.angelfire.com/ky/astronomy)

This space and star Web site provides numerous links to information on stars, constellations, galaxies, nebulae, and more.

- Math in Daily Life (www.learner.org/exhibits/dailymath/)

This site explores how people use math in daily life. Students can test their decision-making skills by deciding whether buying or leasing a new car is right for them and by predicting how much money they can save for their retirement by using an interest calculator.

- The Mid-Atlantic Eisenhower Consortium (www2.rbs.org/)

The Mid-Atlantic Eisenhower Consortium addresses three objectives: coordinating resources through collaboration among organizations, disseminating exemplary materials, and assisting educators in implementing improved curriculum and instruction practices. These objectives are addressed through consortium staff activities in the region as well as nationally, and through consortium team programs in each state. The consortium publishes a newsletter, *Currents,* which maintains a Web site. In conjunction with consortium staff, state teams design and conduct professional development and other activities, which meet the needs of their particular state.

- Mrs. Glosser's Math Goodies (www.mathgoodies.com)

Mrs. Glosser's Math Goodies is a free educational Web site featuring interactive lessons that use a problem-solving approach and actively engage students in the learning process.

- National Center for Science Education (www.natcenscied.org)

Information and resources on evolution education, increasing public understanding of evolution, and coping with the evolution/creation science controversy.

- National Institute for Science Education (www.wcer.wisc.edu/nise)

The National Institute for Science Education (NISE) is funded by the National Science Foundation, the goal of which is to determine the best practices in professional development for teachers of science and mathematics education and to provide information about systemic reform.

- Global SchoolNet (www.globalschoolnet.org/about/index.html)

Global SchoolNet (GSN) combines smart teaching ideas with Web publishing, video conferencing, and other online tools that bridge geographic gaps, allowing young people around the world to learn together. GSN is a growing international network of 90,000+ online educators, who engage in online project-based learning activities. Since its inception, GSN has reached more than a million students from 45,000 schools across 194 countries.

GSN seeks opportunities to partner with schools, universities, communities, businesses, and other organizations to codevelop free or low-cost programs to help students become literate and responsible global citizens and to prepare them for the workforce.

GSN is a 501(c)(3) not-for-profit education organization.

- Industry Initiatives for Science and Math Education (http://www.iisme.org/)

Industry Initiatives for Science and Math Education (IISME) was founded in 1985 by a consortium of San Francisco Bay Area companies in partnership with the Lawrence Hall of Science at the University of California at Berkeley. IISME seeks to transform teaching and learning through industry-education partnerships. They provide teachers with experiences and tools they need to adapt their practices and change their schools so that all students are prepared to be lifelong learners, responsible citizens, and productive employees.

IISME exists to address the critical need for a strong, highly skilled workforce in mathematics, science, and technological fields. This industry-education partnership focuses on teachers as the primary agents for effecting meaningful change in mathematics and science education.

- The Educator's Reference Desk (www.eduref.org/Virtual/Lessons/)

This collection contains more than 2,000 unique lesson plans, which were written and submitted by teachers from all over the United States and the world. These lesson plans are also included in GEM (see following), which links to more than 40,000 online education resources.

- GEM (www.thegateway.org/)

GEM is a 700-member consortium effort to provide educators with quick and easy access to thousands of educational resources found on various federal, state, university, nonprofit, and commercial Internet sites.

- Innovation Station Elementary (www.iteaconnect.org/Networking/IS/IS.htm)

Designed for the International Technology Education Association's (ITEA's) newest learning community—elementary educators—this Web site is for those interested in bringing out every student's creative ability to design, build, tinker, and construct. Innovation Station is for teachers who want to get their students actively involved in learning. It's a teacher's resource for answers, ideas, and teaching techniques that work! This is free to anyone who is passionate about teaching.

- ITEA's Ready-to-Use Classroom Activities! (www.iteaconnect.org/Forms/HitsKitsOnlineForm.htm)

This series of activity guides is designed to supplement *Standards for Technological Literacy: Content for the Study of Technology* (Dugger, 2000) through the use of classroom activities. The activities are directly linked to recommended K–12 courses and present a variety of contemporary methods that infuse recent research concerning learning and teaching. Each of these activities provides detailed guidance for teacher preparation and implementation. They include ready-to-duplicate student handouts and reflection questions and provide multiple assessment strategies.

- PBS Teacher Source (www.pbs.org/teachersource)

This Web site features lessons and activities teachers can use in their classrooms.

- Rainforest Action Network (www.ran.org)

The Rainforest Action Network is a nonprofit environmental organization. This Web site contains an eight-step guide explaining how children can get involved in saving endangered rain forests. The site also features a question-and-answer forum about rain forest deforestation. Other sections contain information about the animals of the rain forest.

- Resource Center of the Environmental and Occupational Health Sciences Institute (www.eohsi.rutgers.edu/rc)

This site offers award-winning environmental health sciences curricular materials and teacher training initiatives for grades K–12. The materials were developed by scientists and researchers and integrate easily into existing lessons. The Resource Center, the outreach component of the Environmental and Occupational Health Sciences Institute (EOHSI), is working to improve environmental health literacy and decision-making skills. The Resource Center has developed resources and training programs from leading scientific research that offer current health science information. Materials and programs address priority environmental and occupational health concerns, integrate new technology and teaching methodologies, and assist teachers in meeting emerging education standards.

- Scientific American Frontiers (www.pbs.org/saf)

Scientific American Frontiers is a prime-time PBS series hosted by Alan Alda. The Web site contains features for teachers and students, video rights, and transcripts. The features are updated regularly and reflect programs that can be seen on TV. These features are a good resource for a PBL project that relates to one of the *Scientific American Frontiers* programs.

- teachers@work (http://teachers.work.co.nz)

More than 3,000 reviewed and rated Internet sites for K–12 educators, separated into curriculum areas. All of the sites have met a set of quality criteria based on authenticity, navigability, content, and relevancy, making them a great choice for research sources.

- wNetSchool (www.thirteen.org/teach/index.html)

wNetSchool, Thirteen/WNET's practical service for K–12 educators, is designed by teachers for teachers. This site offers original Web-based lesson plans, software samples, site reviews, and more.

Bibliography

Albanese, M. A., & Mitchell, S. (1993). Problem-based learning: A review of literature on its outcomes and implementation issues. *Academic Medicine 68*(1):52–81.

Alper, L., Findel, D., Fraser, S., & Resek, D. (1996). Problem-based mathematics not just for the college-bound. *Educational Leadership 53*(8):18–21.

Appleton, K. (1993). Using theory to guide practice: Teaching science from a constructivist perspective. *School Science and Mathematics 93*(5):269–274.

Armstrong, T. (1994). *Multiple intelligences in the classroom.* Alexandria, VA: Association for Supervision and Curriculum Development.

Aspy, D. N., Aspy, C. B., & Quinby, P. N. (1993). What doctors can teach teachers about problem-based learning. *Educational Leadership 50*(7):22–24.

Baroody, A. J. (1998). *Fostering children's mathematical power: An investigative approach to K8 mathematics instruction.* Mahwah, NJ: Lawrence Erlbaum.

Battista, M. T. (1999). The mathematical miseducation of America's youth: Ignoring research and scientific study in education. *Phi Delta Kappan 80*(6):424–433.

Bereiter, C. (2002). *Education and mind in the knowledge age.* Mahwah, NJ: Lawrence Erlbaum.

Blume, R., & Archer, J. (Eds.). (1996). *A handbook for student performance assessment in an era of restructuring.* Reston, VA: Association for Supervision and Curriculum Development.

Boix-Mansilla, V., & Gardner, H. (1997). Of kinds of disciplines and kinds of understanding. *Phi Delta Kappan 78*(5):381–386.

Boud, D., & Feletti, G. (1991). *The challenge of problem-based learning.* New York: St. Martin's.

Brooks, J. G., & Brooks, M. G. (1993). *In search of understanding: The case for constructivist classrooms.* Alexandria, VA: Association for Supervision and Curriculum Development.

Bruner, J. S. (1986). *Actual minds, possible worlds.* Cambridge, MA: Harvard University Press.

Caine, R. N., & Caine, G. (1994). *Making connections: Teaching and the human brain.* Alexandria, VA: Association for Supervision and Curriculum Development.

Caine, R. N., & Caine, G. (1997a). *Education on the edge of possibility.* Menlo Park, CA: Addison-Wesley.

Caine, R. N., & Caine, G. (1997b). *Unleashing the power of perceptual change: The potential of brain-based teaching.* Alexandria, VA: Association for Supervision and Curriculum Development.

Caine, G., Caine, R., & McClintic, C. (2002). Guiding the innate constructivist. *Educational Leadership 60*(1):70–73.

Casey, M., & Tucker, E. (1994). Problem-centered classrooms. *Phi Delta Kappan 10*(94):139–143.

Cheek, D. (1992). *Thinking constructively about science, technology and society education.* Albany: State University of New York Press.

Clarke, J. (1997). Solving problems. In J. Clarke & R. M. Agne (Eds.), *Interdisciplinary high school teaching.* Boston: Allyn & Bacon.

Clarke, J. H., Sanborn, S. D., Aiken, J. A., Cornell, N. A., Goodman, J. B., & Hess, K. K. (1998). *Real questions, real answers: Focusing teacher leadership on school improvement.* Alexandria, VA: Association for Supervision and Curriculum Development.

Cohen, E. G. (1994). *Designing groupwork: Strategies for the heterogeneous classroom,* 2nd ed. New York: Teachers College Press.

Cornbleth, C. (1998). Curriculum in and out of context. *Journal of Curriculum and Supervision 3*(2):85–96.

Costa, A. L., & Kallick, B. (1992). Reassessing assessment. In A. L. Costa, J. A. Bellanca, & R. Fogarty (Eds.), *If minds matter: A Foreword to the future,* Vol. II. Palatine, IL: IRI/Skylight Publishing.

Cowley, G., & Underwood, A. (1998). Memory. *Newsweek 131*(24):48–49, 51–54.

Dearing, B. (2004, November). A call for change in technology education. *Technology Teacher.* Available at www.findarticles.com/p/articles/mi_go2084/is_200411/ai_n9744811

Dehaene, S. (1997). *The number sense: How the mind creates mathematics.* New York: Oxford University Press.

Delisle, R. (1997). *How to use problem-based learning in the classroom.* Alexandria, VA: Association for Supervision and Curriculum Development.

Dennick, R., & Exley, K. (2004). *Small group teaching.* New York: Routledge Falmer.

Dewey, J. (1944). *Democracy and education.* New York: Free Press. (Original work published 1916)

Diamond, M., & Hopson, J. (1998). *Magic trees of the mind: How to nurture your child's intelligence, creativity, and healthy emotions from birth through adolescence.* New York: Dutton-Penguin Putnam.

Dossey, J. A. (1992). The nature of mathematics: Its role and its influence. In D. A. Grouws (Ed.), *Handbook of research on mathematics teaching and learning* (pp. 39–48). New York: Macmillan.

Dossey, J. A. (1997). Defining and measuring quantitative literacy. In L. A. Steen (Ed.), *Why numbers count: Quantitative literacy for tomorrow's America.* New York: College Entrance Examination Board.

Drake, S. M. (1993). *Planning integrated curriculum: The call to adventure.* Alexandria, VA: Association for Supervision and Curriculum Development.

Duckworth, E. (1979, August). Either we're too early and they can't learn it, or we're too late and they know it already: The dilemma of applying Piaget. *Harvard Educational Review 49*:3.

Duffy, T. M., & Johassen, D. H. (Eds). (1992). *Constructivism and the technology of instruction: A conversation.* Hillsdale, NJ: Lawrence Erlbaum.

Dugger, W. (2000). Standards for technological literacy: Content for the study of technology. *Technology Teacher, 59*(5): 8–13.

Evensen, D., & Hmelo, C. (2000). *Problem-based learning: A research perspective on learning interactions.* Mahwah, NJ: Lawrence Erlbaum.

Finkle, S. L., & Torp, L. L. (1995). *Introductory documents.* (Available from the Center for Problem-Based Learning, Illinois Math and Science Academy, 1500 West Sullivan Road, Aurora, IL 60506-1000.)

Flores, A., Middleton, J., Knapp, J., & Staley, F. (1997). *Authentic integration of technology in science and mathematics teacher education.* Submitted to the National Science Foundation at Arizona State University in Tempe, AZ.

Florio-Ruane, S. (1998). Instructional conversations in learning to write and learning to teach. In B. F. Jones & L. Idol (Eds.), *Dimensions of thinking and cognitive instruction: Implications for educational reform*. Hillsdale, NJ: Lawrence Erlbaum.

Forman, S. L., & Steen, L. A. (1999). *Beyond eighth grade: Functional mathematics for life and work*. Berkeley, CA: National Center for Research in Vocational Education.

Franklin, J. (2005, June). Mental mileage: How teachers are putting brain research to work. *ASCD Education Update 47*: 6.

Gallagher, S. A., Rosenthal, H., & Stepien, W. (1992). The effects of problem-based learning on problem-solving. *Gifted Child Quarterly 36*(4):195–200.

Gallagher, S. A., Sher, B. T., Stepien, W. J., & Workman, D. (1995). Implementing problem-based learning in science classrooms. *School Science and Mathematics 95*(3):136–146.

Gardner, H. (1983). *Frames of mind: Theory of multiple intelligences*. New York: Basic Books.

Gardner, H. (1991). *The unschooled mind: How children think and how schools should teach*. New York: Basic Books.

Gardner, H. (1992). *Art, mind and brain: A cognitive approach to creativity*. New York: Basic Books.

Gardner, H. (1993). *Multiple intelligences: The theory in practice*. New York: Basic Books.

Gardner, H. (2005, May). *Multiple lenses on the mind*. Paper presented at the ExpoGestion Conference, Bogota, Columbia.

Goodchild, S. (1992). Active learning, reflection and interpretation. *Mathematics Education Review 1*(3):24–29.

Gorman, C. (1995). How gender may bend your thinking. *Time 146*(3):51.

Greenough, W. T., Briones, T. L., & Klintsova, A.Y. (2004, August 20). Stability of synaptic plasticity in the adult rat visual cortex induced by complex environment exposure. *Brain Research 1018*(1):130–135.

Greenough, W. T., Withers, G. S., & Anderson, B. J. (1992). Experience-dependent synaptogenesis as a plausible memory mechanism. In I. Gormezano & E. A. Wasserman (Eds.), *Learning and memory: The behavioral and biological substrates*. Hillsdale, NJ: Lawrence Erlbaum.

Hart, L. (1985). *Human brain, human learning*. New York: Longman.

Hendley, V. (1996, October). Let problems drive the learning. *AESS Prism*, pp. 30–36.

International Society for Technology in Education. (1998). *National educational technology standards project*. Eugene, OR: ISTE.

International Technology Education Association. (1995). *Technology for all Americans: A rationale and structure for the study of technology*. Reston, VA: International Technology Education Association.

Jensen, E. (1998). *Teaching with the brain in mind*. Alexandria, VA: Association of Supervision and Curriculum Development.

Jensen, E. (2005). *Teaching with the brain in mind* (2nd ed.). Alexandria, VA: Association of Supervision and Curriculum Development.

Johnson, D. W., & Johnson, R. T. (1995). Cooperative versus competitive efforts and problem solving. *Review of Educational Research 65*(2):129–143.

Lemonick, M. (1995). Glimpses of the mind. *Time 146*(3):44–51.

Lowery, L. (1998). Curriculums reflect brain research. *Educational Leadership 56*(3):26–30.

Mathematical Sciences Education Board. (1995). *Mathematical preparation of the technical workforce*. Washington, DC: Mathematical Sciences Education Board.

Michael, J., & Modell, H. (2003). *Active learning in secondary and college science classrooms: A working model for helping the learner to learn*. Mahwah, NJ: Lawrence Erlbaum.

Moon, J. (2004). *A handbook of reflective and experiential learning: Theory and practice.* New York: Routledge.

Musial, D. (1996). Designing assessments in a problem-based learning context. *Problem Log 1*(2):4–5.

Nagel, N. G. (1996). *Learning through real-world problem solving: The power of integrative teaching.* Thousand Oaks, CA: Corwin Press.

Naidu, S. (Ed.). (2003). *Learning and teaching with technology: Principles and practices.* London: Kogan.

Nash, M., Park, A., & Wilwerth, J. (1995). Consciousness may be an evanescent illusion. *Time 146*(3):52.

National Center for Educational Statistics Third International Mathematics and Science Study. (1998). *Pursuing excellence: A study of U.S. fourth, eighth, and twelfth grade mathematics and science achievement in international context.* Washington, DC: Author.

National Commission on Excellence in Education. (1983). *A nation at risk: The imperative for educational reform.* Washington, DC: U.S. Department of Education.

National Council of Teachers of English. (1996). *Standards for English/Language arts.* Urbana, IL: Author.

National Council of Teachers of Mathematics. (1989). *Curriculum and evaluation standards for school mathematics.* Reston, VA: NCTM.

National Council of Teachers of Mathematics. (2000). *Principles and standards for school mathematics.* Reston, VA: Author.

National Research Council. (1989). *Everybody counts: A report to the nation on the future of mathematics education.* Washington, DC: National Academy Press.

National Research Council. (1995). *National science education standards.* Washington, D.C.: National Academy Press.

National Research Council. (1996). *A sampler of national science education standards.* Washington, DC: National Academy Press.

National Research Council. (2000). *How people learn: Brain, mind experience and school.* Washington, DC: National Academy Press.

Nelson, G. (1999). Science literacy for all in the 21st century. *Educational Leadership 57*(2):14–17.

Norman, G. R., & Schmidt, H. G. (1992). The psychological basis of problem-based learning: A review of the evidence. *Academic Medicine 67*(9):557–565.

O'Brien, T. C. (1999). Parrot math. *Phi Delta Kappan 80*(6):434–438.

Orpwood, G., & Garden, R. A. (1998). Assessing mathematics and science literacy. *TIMSS Monograph* No. 4.1. Vancouver, CA: Pacific Educational Press.

Palinscar, A. S., & Brown, A. L. (1989). Classroom dialogues to promote self-regulated comprehension. In J. Brophy (Ed.), *Teaching for understanding and self-regulated learning*, Vol. 1. Greenwich, CT: JAI Press.

Palinscar, A. S., Ramson, K., & Derber, S. (1988/1989). Collaborative research and development of reciprocal teaching. *Educational Leadership 46*(4):37–40.

Papert, S. (1996). *The connected family: Bridging the digital generation gap.* Marietta, GA: Longstreet.

Pate, P. E., Homestead, E. R., & McGinnis, K. L. (1997). *Making integrated curriculum work: Teachers, students, and the quest for coherent curriculum.* New York: Teachers College Press.

Perkins, D. (1992). *Smart schools: From training memories to educating minds.* New York: Free Press.

Perkins, D. (1998). Teaching for understanding. *American Educator 17*(3):8.

Piaget, J. (1952). *The origins of intelligence.* New York: International Universities Press.

Piaget, J. (1954). *The construction of reality in the child.* New York: Ballantine Books.

Pollack, H. (1997). Solving problems in the real world. In L. A. Steen (Ed.), *Why numbers count: Quantitative literacy for tomorrow's America* (pp. 91–105). New York: College Entrance Examination Board.

Popham, W. J. (2001). *The truth about testing: An educator's call to action.* Alexandria, VA: Association of Supervision and Curriculum Development.

Popham, W. J. (2002). Teaching to the test: An expression to eliminate. *Educational Leadership 62*(3):82–83.

Price, G. (1997). Quantitative literacy across the curriculum. In L. A. Steen (Ed.), *Why numbers count: Quantitative literacy for tomorrow's America* (pp. 155–160). New York: College Entrance Examination Board.

Ratey, J. (2001). *A user's guide to the brain: Perception, attention, and the four theaters of the brain.* New York: Pantheon.

Restak, R. M. (1980). *The brain: The last frontier.* New York: Warner.

Ronis, D. (2006). *Brain-compatible mathematics.* Thousand Oaks, CA: Corwin Press.

Ronis, D. (2007). *Brain-compatible assessments.* Thousand Oaks, CA: Corwin Press.

Rowe, M. B. (Ed.). (1990). *What research says to the science teacher*, Vol. 6: *The process of knowing.* Washington, DC: National Science Teachers Association.

Ruiz-Primo, M., & Shavelson, R. (1996). Rhetoric and reality in science performance assessments: An update. *Journal of Research in Science Teaching 33*(4):1046.

Savery, J. R., & Duffy, T. M. (1995). Problem-based learning: An instructional model and its constructivist framework. *Educational Technology 35*(5):31–35.

Schmidt, W. (1996). Press release on 7/8 Grade Achievement by William H. Schmidt, National Research Coordinator for the United States Third International Mathematics and Science Study.

Simon, M. A., Tzur, R., Heinz, K., Kinzel, M., & Smith, M. S. (2000). Characterizing a perspective underlying the practice of mathematics teachers in transition. *Journal for Research in Mathematics Education 37*(5), 579–601.

Sowder, J. T., Philipp, R. A., Armstrong, B. E., & Schappelle, B. P. (1998). *Middle-grade teachers' mathematical knowledge and its relationship to instruction: A research monograph.* Albany: State University of New York Press.

Steen, L. A. (1990). Numeracy. *Daedalus 119*(20):211–231.

Steen, L. A. (1997). *Why numbers count: Quantitative literacy for tomorrow's America.* New York: College Board.

Stepien, W. J., & Gallagher, S. A. (1993). Problem-based learning: As authentic as it gets. *Educational Leadership 50*(7):25–28.

Stepien, W. J., Gallagher, S. A., & Workman, D. (1993). Problem-based learning for traditional and interdisciplinary classrooms. *Journal for the Education of the Gifted 16*(4):338–357.

Stonewater, J. K. (2005, January). Inquiry teaching and learning: The best math class study. *School Science and Mathematics.* Available at http://www.findarticles.com/p/articles/mi_qa3667/is_200501/ai_n9467815

Stonewater, J. K., & Wanko, J. J. (2000). *Challenges and support: Inquiry teaching and learning in mathematics.* Columbus: Ohio Board of Regents, Mathematics and Science Course Development.

Swerdlow, J. (1995). Quiet miracles of the brain. *National Geographic 187*(6):2–41.

Sylwester, R. (1995). *A celebration of neurons: An educator's guide to the human brain.* Alexandria, VA: Association for Supervision and Curriculum Development.

Sylwester, R. (1998). *Student brains, school issues: A collection of articles.* Thousand Oaks, CA: Corwin Press.

Sylwester, R. (1999). The heart of our brain: Exploring key body/brain properties. Presentation article. Phoenix: National Schools Conference Institute.

Sylwester, R. (2004). *How to explain a brain: An educator's handbook of brain terms and cognitive processes.* Thousand Oaks, CA: Corwin Press.

Technical Education Research Centers. (1996). *Investigation in number, data, and space.* White Plains, NY: Dale Seymour Publications.

Torp, L., & Sage, S. (2002). *Problems as possibilities: Problem-based learning for K–16 education.* Alexandria, VA: Association for Supervision and Curriculum Development.

Trends in International Mathematics and Science Study. (2003). Available at http://nces.ed.gov/timss/

Trowbridge, L., & Bybee, R. (1995). *Becoming a secondary school science teacher.* Upper Saddle River, NJ: Prentice Hall.

Trowbridge, L., & Bybee, R. (1996). *Teaching secondary school science.* Upper Saddle River, NJ: Merrill.

Tucker, A., Fey, J., Schifter, D., & Sowder, J. (2001). *The mathematical education of teachers.* Washington, DC: Conference Board of the Mathematical Sciences.

U.S. Department of Education. (2000). *Before it's too late: A report to the nation from the National Commission on Mathematics and Science Teaching for the 21st Century.* Washington, DC: Author.

Vernon, D., & Blake, R. (1993). Does problem-based learning work? A meta-analysis of evaluative research. *Academic Medicine 7*(4):550–563.

Wanko, J. J. (2003, April). *Building preservice teachers' problem solving abilities.* Paper presented at the annual meeting of the National Council of Teachers of Mathematics, San Antonio, TX.

Wanko, J. J., Johnson, I. D., Keiser, J. M., & Stonewater, J. K. (2001). *Middle childhood mathematics inquiry learning project.* Columbus: Ohio Board of Regents, Project SUSTAIN.

West, S. A. (1992). Problem-based learning—A viable addition for secondary school science. *School Science Review 73*(265):47–55.

Wiggins, G. (1989). A true test: Toward more authentic and equitable assessment. *Phi Delta Kappan 70*(2):703–713.

Wiggins, G. (1992). Creating tests worth taking. *Educational Leadership 49*(8):26–33.

Wiggins, G., & Jacobs, H. (1995). *Toward student understanding: Designing coherent curriculum, assessment, and instruction.* Presented at the Restructuring Your School: Integrated/Thematic Curriculum and Performance Assessment Conference. National School Conference Institute, St. Louis, MO. November 30–December 3.

Wiggins, G., & McTighe, J. (2005). *Understanding by design,* exp. 2nd ed. Alexandria, VA: Association for Supervision and Curriculum Development.

Wilkins, J. (2000, December). Preparing for the 21st century: The status of quantitative literacy in the United States. *School Science and Mathematics.* Available at www.findarticles.com/p/articles/mi_qa3667/is_200012/ai_n8904088

Wolfe, P. (1998). Revisiting effective teaching. *Educational Leadership 56*(3):61–64.

Wolfe, P. (2001). *Brain matters: Translating research into classroom practice.* Alexandria, VA: Association for Supervision and Curriculum Development.

Wolfe, P., & Brandt, R. (1998). What do we know from brain research? *Educational Leadership 56*(3):8–13.

Zull, J. (2002). *The art of changing the brain: Enriching the practice of teaching by exploring the biology of learning.* Sterling, VA: Stylus.

Index

Active learning, ix, xiii, 6, 8, 25, 26, 37–38
Adaptation, vii
Alliance to Save Energy, 137–138
Allstate Foundation, 118
Analytical reading, 9
Annenberg/CPB Channel, 138
Apple Computer, 11
Architectural design lesson, 108
    communications tools, 111
    mathematical content standards, 108–110
    performance task for, 111
    problem-solving/decision-making tools, 111
    productivity tools, 111
    project evaluation for, 114–116,
        115–116 (figures)
    project instructions for, 111–114,
        112–113 (figures)
    research tools, 111
    science content standards, 110
    standards for, 108–111
    technology foundation standards,
        110–111
Assessment, 93–94
    alternative assessments, 94–96
    architectural design lesson,
        114–116, 115–116 (figures)
    authentic performance assessments,
        94–95
    benchmark exemplars, 99–100
    constructivist approach and, 31–33
    group project presentations,
        106 (figure), 107
    observation checklists, 104–105,
        104 (figure)
    portfolios, 105, 106 (figure)
    rubrics for, 81, 82–83 (figures), 96–99
    self-evaluation rubrics, 100–104,
        101–103 (figures)
    self-reflective assessment activities, 9, 57
    See also Feedback; Rubrics
Aural materials, 47
Authentic performance assessments, 94–95
Authentic problem situations, viii, 7, 9, 34,
    36–37, 128
    See also Messy problems
AutoZone Partners in Education, 119

Benchmark exemplars, 99–100
Biological Science Curriculum Study
    (BSCS), 29
Brain-compatible learning, 25
    authentic assessments and, 94–95
    constructivist learning theory and, 25–27
    instructional styles, brain development
        and, 28
    integrated activity and, 58–59
    personal meaning making and, 26–27
    problem-based learning and, 27–28
    safe environments and, 25, 27
    See also Brain function; Constructivism;
        Problem-based learning (PBL);
        Problem-based learning classroom
        instruction
Brain function, vii-viii, ix, x
    enriched environments, neural
        organization and, 13–14
    instruction, brain development and, 28
    knowledge construction and, 14
    meaning, search for, 6
    multiple instructional modalities and, 14
    problem-based learning and, 25–28
    See also Brain-compatible learning;
        Constructivism
Bridge building lesson, 71
    communications tools, 74
    mathematics content standards for, 71–73
    performance task for, 75, 75 (figure)
    presentation phase for, 76, 77 (figure)
    problem-solving/decision-making
        tools, 75
    productivity tools, 74
    project extension for, 76
    research tools, 74–75
    resources for, 76
    science content standards for, 73–74
    standards for, 71–75
    technology foundation standards for,
        74–75
    vocabulary development and, 76,
        78 (figure)
Briones, T. L., 13
Business Coalition for Education
    Reform, 122

Business-education partnerships. *See* National Association of Partners in Education (NAPE)
Business plan development, 41–42 (figures)

Caine, G., ix
Car project lesson, 128
    communications tools, 131
    mathematics content standards, 128–130
    performance task for, 131–132
    presentation evaluation for, 132, 133–135 (figures)
    problem-solving/decision-making tools, 131
    productivity tools, 131
    research tools, 131
    science content standards, 130
    standards for, 128–131
    technology foundation standards, 130–131
Case studies, 48, 51, 51 (figure)
Clear questions, 85
Coaching behaviors, 57
Coalition for Community Schools, 122
Cognition, 26, 29, 58–59
Collaborative work, vii, 2, 9, 14, 27, 57–58
Communication literacy, 4–5, 14, 30–31, 33–34
Communications tools, 17, 40, 62, 74, 90, 111, 131
Community-based learning, xi, 14, 36–37, 117
    authentic problems and, 128
    car project lesson, 128–135
    experts from the community and, 126–128
    Internet information resources for, 137–141
    national education coalitions and, 122
    organizational partnerships in education, 125–126
    partnership development process and, 122–123
    school-community partnerships and, 117–118
    service learning activities, 118
    See also National Association of Partners in Education (NAPE)
Complexity, vii
    enriched environments, brain function and, 13–14
    messy/complex problems, ix-x, 1, 6–7
    See also Problem-based learning (PBL)
Comprehension, vii, viii, ix
    multiple instructional modalities and, 14, 33
    spiral/recursive experience and, 29
    written/oral communication literacy and, 4–5
    See also Deep understanding; Problem-based learning classroom instruction

Computer technology, xiii
    technical literacy and, 4
    technology standards and, 10–13
    See also Internet resources; Technical literacy; Technology age
Concept maps, 26
Connect America, 122
Constructive feedback, 6, 32–33
Constructivism, 8, 13–14, 25
    authentic assessments and, 95
    brain-compatible learning and, 25–28
    cognition, principles of, 26, 29
    elaboration phase and, 31, 32
    engagement phase and, 29–30
    evaluation phase and, 31–33
    explanation phase and, 30–31
    exploration phase and, 30
    five E's model of, 29–33
    personal meaning making and, 26–27
    prior knowledge and, 26
    problem-based classroom instruction, 33–38, 33–35 (figures)
    problem-based learning, characteristics of, 27–28
Contextualized problems, vii, ix
    learning links and, x
    See also Integrated approach; Literacy; Problem-based learning (PBL)
Contrived direct experience, 46
Conventional teaching, ix, x, 2, 9, 14, 26, 57
Cooperative learning, 9, 14
Corporation for National Service, 119
Cost estimate plan, 43–44 (figure)
Creative thinking, viii, 8, 26, 36
Critical thinking skills, vii, viii, 2, 8–9
Curiosity, viii
Curriculum and Evaluation Standards for School Mathematics, 4

Decision-making tools, 18, 41, 63, 75, 90, 111, 131
Deep understanding, vii, viii, ix, 14, 26–27, 29, 33, 37
Dehaene, S., ix
Demonstrations, 46
Dewey, J., 45
Dialogue, 33–34
Diamond, M., ix
Direct experience, 46
Divergent questions, 85
Dramatic participation, 46
Duckworth, E., 28, 29

Education Leaders Consortium, 122
Education reform, vii, ix
    school-community partnerships, 117–118
    standards-based instructional policies and, xi-xii
    teaching practices, shift in, 58–59
Educator's Reference Desk, 140
Elaboration process, 31, 32

Emotionality, 25, 27
Engagement process, 29–30, 37–38, 45
Enriched environments, 13–14, 29
Entrepreneurial skill development lesson, 38
    business plan development,
          41–42 (figures)
    communications tools, 40
    cost estimate plan, 43–44 (figure)
    mathematics content standards for, 38–39
    performance task for, 41
    presentation phase, 44
    productivity tools, 40
    project instructions for, 41–42,
          41–44 (figures)
    research tools, 40–41
    resources for, 44
    science content standards for, 39–40
    standards for, 38–41
    technology foundation standards
          for, 40–41
Epsilon Pi Tau, 138
Evaluation process, 31–33, 93–94
    See also Assessment; Feedback; Rubrics
Exhibits, 46
Experiences, 46
    enriched environments, 13, 29
    hands-on activities, xiii, 2, 38
    knowledge construction and,
          13–14, 26–27
    See also Prior knowledge; Real-world
          problems
Experts from the community, 126–128
Explore the Universe, 138
ExxonMobil Foundation, 119

Facilitator role, 1, 7–8, 10, 30–31
    coaching behaviors, 57
    modeling behaviors, 57
    See also Problem-based classroom
          instruction; Problem-based
          learning implementation
Feedback, 6, 32–33, 57
Finkle, S. L., 6
Five E's model of constructivism, 29
    elaboration stage, 31
    engagement stage, 29–30
    evaluation stage, 31–32
    explanation stage, 30–31
    exploration stage, 30
    See also Constructivism
Florio-Ruane, S., 58
Focusing questions, 85

Gardner, H., 28, 29
Garrett A. Morgan (GAM) Technology and
    Transportation Futures program, 126
GEM, 140
Global SchoolNet (GSN), 139
Globalization, xi
Graphic organizers, 9
Greenough, W. T., 13

Group work, vii, 14, 27, 29, 30, 37,
    106 (figure), 107
Guided inquiry, 30

Hands-on activities, xiii, 2, 38
Hein, G., 28
High school:
    architectural design lesson, 108–116
    bridge building lesson, 71–78
    car project lesson, 128–135
    entrepreneurial skill development lesson,
          38–44
    roller coaster lesson, 59–71
    See also Middle school
Higher-order critical thinking, 8–9, 33
Hopson, J., ix

Idea generation, vii, 10
Implementation. *See* Problem-based
    classroom instruction; Problem-based
    learning implementation
Independent investigation, vii
Inductive format, 9–10
Industry Initiatives for Science and Math
    Education (IISME), 139–140
Information literacy, vii, ix
Information processing, viii, ix, 14, 58–59
Information society, 4–5, 14
Innovation Station Elementary, 140
Inquiry-based learning, vii, viii, ix, 8
    brain development and, 28
    guided inquiry, 30
    inquiry-solution method, 8
    instructional environment, characteristics
          of, 37
    socialization/emotionality and, 27
    See also Brain-compatible learning;
          Constructivism; Problem-based
          learning (PBL); Problem-based
          learning implementation
Inquiry contract, 48, 49–50 (figures)
Instruction:
    brain development and, 28
    constructivist theory and, 25–27
    conventional format for, ix, x, 2, 9, 14
    information society and, 4–5
    inquiry-based strategies, viii
    mathematics standards and, 5
    minds-on experience and, xiii
    multiple approaches to, 14, 25
    problem-based classroom and, 33–38,
          33–35 (figures)
    recursive/spiral experience and, 29
    student-centered learning, vii, viii, ix, 9
    teacher-centered perspective, vii, xi, 9
    See also Learning; Mathematics
          instruction; Science instruction;
          Problem-based learning (PBL);
          Problem-based learning
          implementation; Teaching
Instructional leadership, 59

Integrated approach, viii, ix, xii, 58–59
  entrepreneurial skill development
    lesson, 38–44
  math/science, real-world integration
    of, 14
  meteorology lesson, 15–24
  planning for, 79–81, 80 (figure)
  technology standards, math/science
    instruction and, 10–13
  See also Community-based learning;
    Literacy; Problem-based classroom
    instruction; Problem-based learning
    (PBL); Problem-based learning
    implementation
Interactive learning, 13–14
International Partnership Network, 122
International Society for Technology in
  Education (ISTE), viii, xi, xii, 11, 17,
    40, 62, 74, 90, 110, 130
International Technology Education
  Association (ITEA), 11, 140
Internet resources:
  bridge building lesson, 76
  business plan development, 44
  data sources, 10
  information resources for
    math/science/technology, 137–141
  interactive learning and, 13
  Mississippi Delta ecosystem lesson, 92
  National Association of Partners in
    Education, 123
  organizational partnerships in Education,
    125–126
  research activities and, 4
  roller coaster lesson, 71
  service learning/business-education
    partnerships, 118
  technical literacy and, 4
  weather research resources, 19–24
Interpretation, viii
ITEA's Ready-to-Use Classroom
  Activities, 140

Jensen, E., ix
Job skills. *See* Work requirements
Journals, 107, 107 (figure)

Klintsova, A. Y., 13
Knowledge construction, 13–14, 26–27, 34

Laboratory for Student Success (LSS), 125
Learning:
  active learning, ix, xiii, 6, 8, 25, 26, 37–38
  brain-compatible learning, 25–28
  constructivist approach to, 8
  contextualized problems and, vii
  deep understanding and, viii, ix
  enriched environments, brain function
    and, 13–14
  hands-on vs. minds-on engagement
    and, xiii

interactivity and, 13–14
lifelong learning, viii, 4, 9
links in, x
prior knowledge and, vii, xii, 10,
  26, 34, 38
problem-based approach to, viii
reflection/interpretation and, viii
self-directed learning, viii, 2, 6, 8
teacher-centeredness vs.
  student-centeredness, vii
See also Constructivism; Instruction;
  Problem-based learning (PBL)
Lesson planning. *See* Planning
  problem-based learning
Lessons. *See* Middle school; High school
Lifelong learning, viii, 4, 9
Literacy, 2
  mathematical literacy, 2–3
  problem-based learning and, 6–10
  scientific literacy, 3–4
  technical literacy, 4
  written/oral communication literacy, 4–5
Lowery, L., 13, 14

Manipulatives, 9
Materials/resources, 46–47
  See also Community-based learning;
    Internet resources; National
    Association of Partners in Education
    (NAPE)
Math in Daily Life, 138
Mathematical literacy, 2–3
*Mathematical Preparation of the Technical
  Workforce*, x
Mathematics instruction, ix
  computer technology and, xiii
  cyber-age math education, 13–14
  goals, development of, 4–5
  standards for, xi, xii-xiii, 5, 15–16, 38–39,
    59–61, 71–73, 87–89, 108–110,
    128–130
  technology standards and, 10–13
  written/oral communication literacy
    and, 4–5
  See also Entrepreneurial skill development
    lesson; Meteorology lesson;
    Problem-based learning (PBL);
    Science instruction
McClintic, C., ix
McKee Foods, 119
Meaningful learning, vii, 25
  cognition, principles of, 26
  personal meaning making and, 26–27
  prior knowledge and, xii, 26
  problem-based learning and, 6
  reflection/interpretation and, viii
  self-directed learning and, 8
  See also Constructivism; Instruction;
    Learning; Problem-based learning
    (PBL)
Messy problems, ix-x, 1, 6–7, 34, 36–38

Metacognition, 7–8
   authentic assessments and, 96
   constructivist approach and, 25–26
   problem-solving skill development and, 37
   strategies for, 9
   See also Problem-based learning (PBL)
Meteorology lesson, 15
   communications tools, 17
   mathematics content standards for, 15–16
   performance task for, 18, 18 (figure)
   problem-solving/decision-making tools, 18
   productivity tools, 17
   project instructions, 19, 19 (figure)
   research extension activities, 20–24
   research tools, 18
   resources for, 19–24
   science content standards for, 16–17
   standards for, 15–17
   technology foundation standards
      for, 17–18
Metropolitan Life Foundation, 119
Mid-Atlantic Eisenhower Consortium, 138
Middle school:
   architectural design lesson, 108–116
   car project lesson, 128–135
   entrepreneurial skill development lesson,
      38–44
   meteorology lesson, 15–24
   Mississippi Delta ecosystem lesson, 87–92
   roller coaster lesson, 59–71
   See also High school
Milken Exchange on Education
   Technology, 11
Minds-on experience, xiii
Mississippi Delta ecosystem lesson, 87
   communications tools, 90
   mathematics content standards, 87–89
   problem-solving/decision-making tools, 90
   productivity tools, 90
   project task for, 90–92, 91–92 (figure)
   research tools, 90
   resources for, 92
   science content standards, 89
   standards for, 87–90
   technology foundation standards, 90
Modeling behaviors, 57
Mrs. Glosser's Math Goodies, 139
Multiple intelligences, 29, 33

Nation as Risk, A, 117
National Academy of Sciences, 3
National Aeronautics and Space Association
   (NASA), 11
National Alliance for Business, 122
National Association of Partners in
      Education (NAPE), 118
   Allstate Foundation, 118
   AutoZone, 119
   Corporation for National Service, 119
   ExxonMobil Foundation, 119
   McKee Foods, 119

Metropolitan Life Foundation, 119
   national education coalitions and, 122
   participating groups, 118–121
   partnership development process,
      122–123
   publications of, 123–125
   SBC Foundation, 120
   Shell Oil Company Foundation, 120
   United States Department of
      Education, 120
   Verizon, 120
   W. K. Kellogg Foundation, 120
National Business Roundtable's Education
   Task Force, 122
National Center for Education Statistics Third
   International Mathematics and Science
   Study, 37
National Center for Science Education, 139
National Coalition for Parent Involvement in
   Education, 122
National Commission on Excellence
   in Education, 117
National and Community Service
   Coalition, 122
National Council for Accreditation of
   Teacher Education (NCATE), 11
National Council of Teachers of English
   (NCTE), 5
National Council of Teachers of
   Mathematics (NCTM), viii, xi,
   xii-xiii, 4–5, 38, 59, 71, 94, 128
National Educational Technology Standards
   (NETS) Project, xi, xii, 11–13, 17, 40,
   62, 74, 90, 110, 130
National Institute for Science Education, 139
National Science Education Standards
   (NSES), xi, xii, 4, 39, 61, 73, 89,
   94, 110, 130
National Science Foundation, 10–11
National Science Teachers Association
   (NSTA), viii, 3
Norman, G. R., 6
Northeast and Islands Regional Educational
   Laboratory (LAB), 125–126
Northwest Regional Educational Laboratory
   (NWREL), 126
Numeracy. *See* Quantitative literacy

Observation checklists, 104–105,
   104 (figure)
Open-ended questions, 85
Oral communication literacy, 4–5, 14,
   33–34

Papert, S., 8
Participatory dialogue, 33–34
Partnership for Family Involvement in
   Education, 122
Partnerships. *See* Community-based
   learning; National Association of
   Partners in Education (NAPE)

PBS Teacher Source, 140

Performance assessments. *See* Assessments; Rubrics

Piaget, J., 28, 29, 57

Planning problem-based learning, 79
  integrated learning plan, 79–81, 80 (figure), 82 (figure)
  Mississippi Delta ecosystem lesson, 87–92
  project implementation guidelines, 81–84, 83 (figure)
  questioning strategies, 84–86, 86 (figure)

Portfolios, 105, 106 (figure)

Principles and Standards for School Mathematics, viii, xi, xii

Prior knowledge, vii, xii, 10, 26, 34, 38

Problem-based classroom instruction, 33
  active learning experiences and, 37–38
  deep understanding and, 33, 37
  entrepreneurial skill development lesson, 38–44
  environmental characteristics and, 37
  messy problems and, 34, 36–38
  multiple intelligences and, 33
  participatory dialogue, initiation of, 33–34, 33 (figure)
  prior knowledge and, 34
  solution path outline for, 34–36, 35 (figure)
  teacher-centered vs. student-centered teaching and, 33–34, 34 (figure)
  teachers, personal characteristics of, 37
  See also Planning problem-based learning; Problem-based learning (PBL); Problem-based learning implementation

Problem-based learning (PBL), vii-viii, ix
  brain-compatible learning and, 25–28
  constructivist approach to learning and, 8
  critical thinking skill development and, 8–9
  cyber-age math/science education and, 13–14
  feedback and, 6
  inductive format and, 9–10
  interactivity and, 13, 14
  learning links and, x
  literacy, enhancement of, 6–10
  mathematical literacy and, 2–3, 4–5
  messy/complex problems and, ix-x, 1, 6–7
  metacognitive strategies for, 9–10
  minds-on experience and, xiii
  process implementation, difficulties in, 7
  questioning strategies for, 9
  real-life referenced problems, xi
  roles for, 6
  scientific literacy and, 3–4
  self-reflective activities and, 9
  simulations, xi
  student-community problems, xi
  teacher-directed approach, xi

technology standards and, 10–13
written/oral communication literacy and, 4–5
See also Constructivism; Meteorology lesson example; Problem-based classroom instruction; Problem-based learning implementation; Standards

Problem-based learning implementation, 45
  bridge building lesson, 71–78
  case studies and, 48, 51, 51 (figure)
  collaborative classrooms and, 57–58
  facilitator role and, 56–58
  inquiry contract and, 48, 49–50 (figures)
  leadership role and, 59
  phases of implementation, 45–47
  problem analysis and, 47
  problem design and, 46
  questioning strategies, 55–56, 56 (figure)
  resource location/identification and, 46–47
  roller coaster lesson, 59–71
  simulations and, 51–52, 53 (figure)
  teaching practice, shift in, 58–59
  techniques for learning, 47–56
  workshops and, 52, 54–55 (figures)
  See also Planning problem-based learning; Problem-based classroom instruction; Problem-based learning (PBL)

Problem-solving tools, 18, 41, 63, 75, 90, 111, 131

Productivity tools, 17, 40, 62, 74, 90, 111, 131

Professional development, 4, 59

Quantitative literacy, vii, 2–3

Questioning strategies, 9, 55–56, 56 (figure), 84–86, 86 (figure)

Rainforest Action network, 140–141

Reading. *See* Analytical reading

Real-world problems, viii, ix, xi, 36–37, 57
  enriched environments, brain function and, 13, 29
  hands-on vs. minds-on engagement and, xiii
  inquiry-solution learning method and, 8, 9
  knowledge construction and, 13–14, 26–27
  mathematical literacy and, 2–3
  messy/complex problems, ix-x, 1, 6–7, 34, 36–38
  See also Problem-based learning (PBL)

Reflection, viii, 5
  group work and, 29
  self-reflective assessment activities, 9, 96

Reform. *See* Education reform

Regional Education Laboratories
  Internet Resources on Community Partnerships, 125

Research-based methods, vii-viii, ix
Research tools, 18, 40–41, 62–63,
    74–75, 90, 111, 131
Resource Center of the Environmental
    and Occupational Health Sciences
    Institute, 141
Resources. *See* Community-based learning;
    Internet resources; Materials/resources;
    National Association of Partners in
    Education (NAPE)
Roller coaster lesson, 59
    communications tools, 62
    mathematics content standards
        for, 59–61
    performance task for, 63, 63 (figure)
    presentation phase for, 69, 70 (figure)
    problem-solving/decision-making tools, 63
    productivity tools, 62
    project instructions for, 63–69,
        64–65 (figures), 67–69 (figures)
    research tools, 62
    resources for, 71
    science content standards for, 61–62
    standards for, 59–63
    technology foundation standards for,
        62–63
Ronis, D., ix, 18, 19, 27, 35, 41, 42, 44, 50,
    51, 53, 54, 63, 64, 66, 67, 69, 70, 75,
    77, 78, 80, 82, 83, 92, 95, 98, 102,
    103, 104, 112, 113, 133, 134, 135
Rote learning, vii, ix
Rubrics:
    benchmark exemplars and, 99–100
    design process for, 96–97
    evidence of learning, 81, 82–83 (figures)
    group project presentation rubric,
        106 (figure), 107
    journals, 107, 107 (figure)
    levels of performance, 97, 98 (figures)
    portfolio evaluation system, 105,
        106 (figure)
    scoring rubrics, 96–99, 98 (figures)
    self-evaluation rubrics, 100–104,
        101–103 (figures)
Ruiz-Primo, M., 94

Safe environments, 25, 27
SBC Foundation, 120
Scaffolding, 57
Schemata, 26
Schmidt, H. G., 6
School-community partnerships.
    See Community-based learning
Science instruction:
    cyber-age science education, 13–14
    standards for, xi, xii, xiii, 16–17, 39–40,
        61–62, 73–74, 89, 110, 130
    technology standards and, 10–13
    written/oral communication literacy
        and, 4–5

See also Mathematics instruction; Problem-
        based learning (PBL)
Scientific American Frontiers, 141
Scientific literacy, 3–4
Secondary level. *See* High school
Self-directed learners, viii, 2, 6, 8, 38
Self-evaluation rubrics, 100–104,
    101–103 (figures)
Self-reflective assessment, 9, 57, 96,
    101, 105
Self-reliance, vii
Service learning, 118
Shaavelson, R., 94
Shell Oil Company Foundation, 120
Simulations, xi, 51–52, 53 (figure)
Social interaction, vii, ix, 25, 27
Socratic dialogue, 9
Solution path outline, 34–36, 35 (figure)
Standards, xi, xi-xiii
    architectural design lesson, 108–116
    bridge building lesson, 71–75
    car project lesson, 128–131
    entrepreneurial skill development lesson,
        38–41
    instructional policies and, xii
    intent of, xi-xii
    mathematics standards, xii-xiii, 5, 15–16,
        38–39, 59–61, 71–73, 87–89, 110,
        128–130
    meteorology lesson, 15–18
    Mississippi Delta ecosystem lesson, 87–90
    problem-based instruction and, 37
    roller coaster lesson, 59–63
    science standards, xii, 16–17, 39–40,
        61–62, 73–74, 89, 110, 130
    scoring rubric and, 96–99, 98 (figures)
    technology standards, xii, 10–13, 17–18,
        40–41, 62–63, 89–90, 110–111,
        130–131
Strategic writing, 9
Student-centered learning, vii, viii, ix, 9,
    34 (figure), 95
Student-community problems, xi
Sylwester, R., ix

Teacher-centered perspective, vii, xi, 9, 26,
    34 (figure), 58
teachers@work, 141
Teaching:
    conventional approach to, ix, x, 2, 9,
        14, 26, 57
    facilitator role in, 1, 7–8, 10, 30–31,
        56–58
    problem-based learning classrooms
        and, 33–38, 33–35 (figures)
    professional development and, 4, 59
    scaffolding and, 57
    teacher-centered approach, vii, xi, 9,
        26, 34 (figure), 58
    technical literacy and, 4

See also Instruction; Learning;
   Problem-based classroom instruction;
   Problem-based learning (PBL);
   Problem-based learning
   implementation
Teams. *See* Collaborative work; Group work
Technical literacy, 4
   cyber-age math/science instruction and,
      13–14
   grade-level technology standards, 12–13
   See also Technological age; Technology
      standards
Technological age, vii, viii, 2
   job-related skills and, x
   technology foundation standards,
      xi, xii, xiii
   See also Computer technology; Internet
      resources; Problem-based learning
      (PBL); Technical literacy; Technology
      standards
Technology standards, 10–13
   architectural design lesson, 110–111
   car project lesson, 130–131
   entrepreneurial skill development
      lesson, 40–41
   meteorology lesson, 17–18
   Mississippi Delta ecosystem lesson, 90
   roller coaster lesson, 62–63
   See also Technical literacy
Theory development, viii
Thought-provoking questions, 85, 126
Torp, L. L., 6

Transfer of thinking, 9
*Trends in International Mathematics and
   Science Study* (TIMSS), xi

Understanding. *See* Comprehension; Deep
   understanding
U.S. Coast Guard Partnership in Education
   (PIE) Program, 126
U.S. Department of Education, 11, 120

Verizon, 120
Visual materials, 47
Vygotsky, L. S., 57

W. K. Kellogg Foundation, 120
Weather research. *See* Meteorology lesson
   example
Wiggins, G., 94
wNetSchool (WNET), 141
Wolfe, P., ix
Work requirements, vii, ix
   mathematics preparation, x, 4–5
   scientific literacy and, 3–4
   technological age and, 2
Workshops, 52, 54–55 (figures)
Writing. *See* Strategic writing; Written
   communication literacy
Written communication literacy, 4–5, 14
Written materials, 47

Zone of proximal development, 57
Zull, J., ix

CORWIN PRESS

The Corwin Press logo—a raven striding across an open book—represents the union of courage and learning. Corwin Press is committed to improving education for all learners by publishing books and other professional development resources for those serving the field of PreK–12 education. By providing practical, hands-on materials, Corwin Press continues to carry out the promise of its motto: **"Helping Educators Do Their Work Better."**